Teaching the Museum:
Careers in Museum Education

Teaching the Museum: Careers in Museum Education
Edited by Leah M. Melber, Ph.D.

© 2014 The AAM Press

Published by
The AAM Press
American Alliance of Museums
Washington, DC

ISBN 978-1-933253-92-3 (print)
ISBN 978-1-933253-95-4 (e-book)

Teaching the museum : careers in museum education / [edited by] Leah M.
Melber, Ph.D.
    pages cm
  Summary: "Education departments in museums of all kinds serve millions
of students and adult learners every year, using the objects and other
resources of the museum. *Teaching the Museum* offers insights, anecdotes
and valuable advice on how to get started and how to succeed in this
rapidly growing field. Twenty contributors with decades of museum
experience point out the opportunities for new graduates and seasoned
teachers alike"-- Provided by publisher.
  ISBN 978-1-933253-92-3 (pbk.) -- ISBN 978-1-933253-95-4 (ebook)
1. Museums--Vocational guidance. 2. Museums--Employees--Training of.
3. Museum techniques--Study and teaching (Higher) I. Melber, Leah M.
  AM7.T43 2014
  069.07--dc23
                          2013045468

Teaching the Museum: Careers in Museum Education

Edited by Leah M. Melber, Ph.D.

 The AAM Press

Table of Contents

Section 3: When Obstacles Arise

Section 4: Looking Forward

Teaching the Museum: Careers in Museum Education
is published with the generous support of

Introduction

The most helpful career advice I've received over the years usually involved food, drink, a long car ride or some strange twist of fate that landed me in the company of someone I could really learn from. That shared glass of wine at the conference social led to a helpful bit of advice that got me through a rough patch at work. The penny-saving car pool to review a nearby exhibit with someone new from my institution led to stronger working relationships down the road. Four graduate students sharing one double room at an international conference to save pennies, well...that was just plain miserable. I do still collaborate with those ladies even today, 14 years later, so perhaps in the long run it was worth the pain.

Recently, as I've gained a smile line or two, I've noticed more and more emerging professionals asking for my guidance, advice and mentorship. As I began to dole out bits of wisdom I felt might be helpful, I soon noticed a theme. What most of these young professionals were interested in was the informal advice I had to offer. They had experienced excellent grad school instruction, and had tapped into strong professional libraries and journal collections. What they didn't have, however, were those horror stories of our mistakes, right-place, right-time examples, and a cache of real-world advice to pull from and make their own. In short, the things that we are often hesitant to share—be it a fear that shows our fallibility or simply a time so long ago it was forgotten.

So it was late one night in a hotel in Gwalior, India, when I got to think-ing. What if I tapped into the talents of my colleagues and asked them to join me in sharing a key bit of advice with the next generation of educators? There would be no room for academic rhetoric and no mandated citations at the end of each sentence. Their charge would be to pretend they were at a social mixer, speaking in hushed tones, telling it like it really is. And so, with the confidence that comes from jetlag-induced insomnia halfway around the world from my office, I shot off an e-mail to these colleagues with my grand idea. And I woke the next morning, wondering what would come of it all....

And you know what? They all wrote me back. And this book is what they wanted to share.

Leah M. Melber, Ph.D.
Senior Director, Hurvis Center for Learning Innovation and Collaboration
Lincoln Park Zoo, Chicago

Section 1: Climbing the Ladder

Chapter 1

Say "Yes"…and Figure It Out Later

Leah M. Melber, Ph.D.

Senior Director, Hurvis Center for Learning Innovation and Collaboration
Lincoln Park Zoo, Chicago

T he first time I assisted with an exhibit evaluation, it did not start off as a pleasant experience. While still a very new doctoral student in my first semester of coursework, I had come to the project under the guidance of a much more experienced colleague. As I sat in her living room, she piled stacks and stacks of student questionnaires in front of me, with the simple instruction to start on the thematic category construction part of the analysis. I quickly flipped through one stack of forms, looked at her blankly, and quietly asked where the Likert scale rankings were. She laughed and walked out of the room to attend to another matter. I fought the butterflies building in my stomach and made a plan to read ahead in my research methods book later that night. What had I gotten myself into?

Of course, this was just one of many uncomfortable situations that would eventually help me build my professional skill set. And ironically, I still use the methodology I learned from that evaluation experience. But the most important lesson to come out of this situation, and many like it that were to follow, was this philosophy: "Say 'yes'...and figure it out later." The reality is that had I known how different this would be from the experience I possessed at the time, I likely would have said no, out of fear of failure. In this case, I didn't have the opportunity to over-think all the reasons why I shouldn't participate. It never dawned on me that I might not be prepared. Over the years I have stayed with this philosophy, and as opportunities arose for which perhaps I did know enough to have a healthy dose of fear, I learned to avoid focusing on all the reasons I shouldn't accept a new professional opportunity. If I had confidence that I could be even marginally successful, I opted to say "yes" and have confidence that the details would figure themselves out.

There have been numerous times that I found myself saying "yes" while my stomach swam with butterflies: signing my first book contract, accepting my first freelance evaluation, accepting an at-will job across the country in lieu of pursuing tenure, boarding a plane for Vietnam to serve for a month as an educational documentarian of the research process and taking a leadership role in a new type of project. And while each certainly had challenging moments, I can honestly say the eventual benefits far outweighed any of the discomfort I experienced along the way.

One career experience in which this lesson became clear was being part of an exhibition design team for the first time. It was a multi-year project with a significant budget and even more significant challenges that arose throughout the length of the program. Due to staffing changes at the institution, my original responsibilities as part of the team gradually increased and I had the opportunity to say "yes" to new types of project activities that fell outside my original responsibilities. In some cases it was tackling a unique task. In others it was overseeing a task through a new lens, according to a new model or on a scale I had yet to experience. For example, writing a single label in no way prepared me for overseeing label development—and associated contributors and reviewers with often disparate views—for an entire 6,000-square-foot exhibit. I still said "yes" to wrangling that aspect of the project. When it became apparent that we needed voice-over descriptions to align with our goals of universal access,

I quickly said "yes," and to this day derive some pleasure knowing somewhere in this world my detailed oral description of a Natufian burial site will live on. Though I had limited experience with live television, I said "yes" without hesitation to representing the exhibit at an in-studio news interview. Each time I said "yes" to being involved in a new part of the project, I was adding a tool to my professional tool-kit and building my expertise in new and interesting ways.

Of course as I describe the opportunity years later, it reads as a fabulous and enjoyable professional learning activity anyone would envy. In reality, it was indeed a fabulous learning opportunity that I am still tapping into today. Enjoyable, however, might not be the best descriptor. For a year I worked nearly daily outside my comfort zone, feeling at any given time frustration with process, fear of personal failure, disappointment with project outcomes and anxiety over meeting production deadlines. It wasn't until long after the project was completed that I realized the benefits I gained from such a rich and complex opportunity. And perhaps most important, learning that "yes" wasn't always going to be comfortable but had the potential to bring extraordinary professional benefits down the road.

The key to this philosophical approach is of course to refrain from indiscriminate use of the word "yes." This is not an excuse to become a professional doormat, or end up overseeing a project at which you honestly cannot succeed. It isn't license to take on an additional work load that you simply cannot handle successfully, or to tackle projects that clearly fall outside your expertise and skill set, such as an education professional agreeing to develop a conservation plan for a set of rare textiles.

It does refer to saying "yes" to opportunities that may be new and frankly uncomfortable as part of an overall plan of personal and professional growth. It means not limiting your future opportunities only to what you have successfully accomplished in the past. It means being willing to take a risk in order to eventually broaden the scope of your expertise and the range of your skill set. It means sometimes failing, but still gaining valuable experience that will ultimately contribute to overall professional growth. It often means striking a balance between striving for perfection and simply striving for success—two very different outcomes. When you say "yes" to new opportunities, you create a professional world that is nearly boundless.

So how best to take advantage of new opportunities in a professionally responsible manner? I've found the following questions invaluable as I determine whether or not to say "yes" to a new opportunity:

1. Is the project a sound one?
2. Do I have the basic expertise needed to succeed?
3. Do I have colleagues or other supportive resources to help me move beyond the expertise I have?
4. Can I see the project through to completion?
5. What could I gain from achieving even moderate success?
6. Are there any serious risks to project involvement from which I could not recover?

The first question is the most critical. As we progress in our careers, we will have the good fortune to hear about many new project ideas and potential initiatives. Spending a few minutes to consider the project and the level of support or backing it has should be your first consideration. Questions two and three ensure the project is indeed one that you are well suited for. You may not have all the building blocks you need, but you will need to have a strong base and a plan for learning what it is you need to know to advance to the next level. Secondly, leaving a project or an assignment unfinished can be more detrimental than not taking on the opportunity in the first place. Be honest with your ability to complete your involvement. Last, risk on return is a critical consideration. Any new opportunity brings risk. The goal is to ensure that the potential rewards outweigh the potential risk associated with participating in the project. Depending on the opportunity, other questions might arise that are important to consider before moving forward.

An example of one of the few times I said "yes" and lived to regret it involved serving as a contributing writer to an environmental curriculum project. I will honestly admit I was blinded by the compensation package and did not carefully move through the questions. If I had, I would have had a decision after question one. Once the full situation became apparent, I was eventually able to extricate myself from the project (question three). Though I was not compensated for all of my writing efforts, I did receive significant compensation in that I learned how to be more discerning when it came to saying "yes."

No matter how many years they have in the field, most museum professionals will tell you that each day brings new learning experiences and opportunities to grow professionally. We all continue to say "yes" to new opportunities that can sometimes reawaken the stomach butterflies we experienced as emerging professionals. More commonly, however, experience has taught us that stretching ourselves professionally can bring incalculable opportunities and rewards. And when we say "yes" to these opportunities, it is one of the greatest gifts we can give to our career. When I say "yes" now, those "nervous butterflies" have been replaced by excitement about where this new opportunity might eventually lead.

Chapter 2

When You Are Offered the Perfect Job You Never Wanted, Take It

Brad Irwin

Senior Learning Engagement Manager
Natural History Museum, London

I've always been career-focused, mapping out what I needed to do to work in the learning department of an art gallery. At the age of 18, I flew from Auckland to Sydney to meet with the head of learning at the Art Gallery of New South Wales to get career advice on how to "climb the ladder." For the next 10 years I followed the advice given and worked in many art galleries developing, delivering and managing learning programs, gaining all the relevant experience and qualifications needed to succeed in the field.

In 2008 I decided to move hemispheres and try my luck in London. I knew I had the experience and expertise to work in one of London's public art galleries, and there were a number of advertised positions that suited me perfectly. Desire and reality, however, are often incompatible beasts, and soon enough application rejection letters piled up whilst my confidence and bank balance were in free-fall. Desperate times called for desperate measures, so instead of focusing on art gallery education, I widened the net and applied for anything that was related to informal learning.

One of the many jobs I applied for was learning operations manager at the Natural History Museum, London. The position involved managing the science educator team and running the daily operations of a complex informal learning program. I've never been wildly passionate about natural history, but many of the criteria for the job matched my skills and experience. My application was successful, and I made it to the interview stage. Interviewing for a job you don't really want is tricky, but I went in presentable, focused and well rehearsed. After a few days I was offered the position, and after much thought I accepted it, though somewhat begrudgingly. I didn't really want to work in a natural history museum, I wasn't that interested in science and the thought of operational management wasn't really part of the grand career plan.

Four years on, I'm still at the museum and the position I didn't want has become a fantastic job full of opportunity, challenge and reward. This has very much led me to the philosophy: "When you are offered the perfect job you never wanted, take it."

I recall my first day at the natural history museum clearly. I remember meeting the science educator team in the morning, feeling like a total fraud. There I was, surrounded by a large bunch of impressive science experts who deliver programs to a wide variety of audiences; I knew very little about the subject matter that they were incredibly passionate about. For the first few months I put my head down. I learned the intricacies of the educational program and got to know my staff. I'd be lying if I said I wasn't looking for other jobs, but there was something about the organization that piqued my interest. The team was a wonderful challenge, my superior was really interested in utilizing my experiences in new and innovative ways, and there was something refreshing about working in a foreign environment, performing tasks that use your skills in a new and exciting way.

It didn't take me long to find my feet, and I began to see how my skills could add value to the museum. Having worked in pre-service teacher training for a number of years, I could see that my experience in observing and feeding back to staff on educational practice would not only assist in their professional development but also add something unique to the sector. I had a great working relationship with my boss, so I shared my thoughts and she was extremely receptive to developing a highly reflective, face-to-face delivery team. After many meetings, our ideas began to take shape and a much larger department-wide project began to emerge. Entitled "Quality Learning at the Natural History Museum," it involved an examination of departmental culture—redeveloping professional development initiatives and finding ways to re-immerse ourselves in educational theory and research; creating a series of processes and procedures to ensure all learning programs were consistent, collaborative, reflective and educationally robust; and creating a framework to ensure front-facing staff were supported in the delivery of learning experiences—promoting and enhancing reflective practice.

The project played to my strengths and past experience, and within six months my role morphed into a mix of activities that I loved doing. I was working with informal researchers to answer questions in our field; developing delivery staff to be the best they could be in a setting that is second to none; and traveling around the world speaking at conferences about our programs and initiatives. Getting that "perfect job" was not without its frustrations. I had a clear idea, however, of what I wanted to achieve and was given the flexibility to develop a framework that benefited my individual position as well as the department as a whole.

I should be careful to note that one needs to approach my philosophy with caution. The term "perfect" is highly subjective. Hindsight is a blessing, and what worked for me might not work for you. So in an attempt to expand on my philosophy, I've created some steps to help you get that perfect job. Failure to follow may (or may not) end in severe disappointment and career disillusionment.

1. **Widen the net.**
   Keep an open mind when looking for a job. Focusing on one institution or a specific sector narrows your options, which may result in you missing some exciting opportunities.

2. **Find museum friends.**
   Research your sector and find several people in the greater museum world who hold positions that interest you. E-mail them and ask if

you can take them out for coffee to get advice and guidance. Most people love free things, so throw in a cake and you'll be amazed how many people will say yes.

3. **Keep moving.**
   No matter what you do or where you work, it is essential that you constantly develop your skills and knowledge base. Look into your organization's human resources department and attend as many courses as you can, go to conferences and learn about the work of other institutions, and read academic journals to get a thorough understanding of the literature that underpins our practice. In this sector it is important you don't "stand still." Instead enrich yourself professionally and move in the direction that you want to go!

4. **Develop professional relationships.**
   If you are currently in a post, then you need to develop a healthy professional relationship with your superiors. Their perception of you is paramount, so make sure you always come across as intelligent, hard working, constructive, full of innovative and relevant ideas. Your boss is also responsible for your professional development and inevitably has a better understanding of opportunities on the horizon, so share your skill set and experience with her or him. If you are completing job activities quickly and accurately, then your boss should see that you have more time to get involved in new opportunities.

5. **Don't over-plan the future.**
   The grand plan "kind of" worked for me. It helped me to develop skills and experience in a certain sector, but it was far too prescriptive, resulting in a target that I didn't achieve. Tal Ben-Shahar, in his book *Happier* (McGraw-Hill, 2007), theorizes that happiness is not achieved through a life-changing event, rather "...it is shaped incrementally, experience by experience, moment by moment" (p. 168). I can't help but think there is something in this, in terms of finding that perfect job. Rather than over-planning the future, point yourself in the right direction, work hard and see what happens!

Variations of my philosophy still guide me today. I still throw myself into opportunities that I'm not that keen on: in the near future I'm going to train to become an official museum coach. Though not sure where this will lead, I am certain that it will add to my skill base. Writing this essay has provided a great opportunity to reflect on my career, and I can't stress enough how important it is to develop yourself professionally, taking risks along the way. I started off with a focused plan, ended up working in an organization that I wasn't that interested in, and now I'm still there, doing a job that I love. I could use so many clichés to illustrate my point, but I think a dear friend summed it up best when she said to me over a glass (or two) of wine, "Take a chance, it's all practice."

Chapter 3

Museum Outsiders and the Value of an External Lens

Kathleen Tinworth

Principal
ExposeYourMuseum LLC

S omehow it always seems to come up. It usually follows innocuous questions like, "How long were you at the Denver Museum of Nature & Science?" or "How long have you been consulting?" or "Where did you do your graduate work?" The truth will come out. It's only a matter of time until I reveal myself as one of our industry's great poseurs—a museum transplant. The truth is, I was only at the Denver Museum of Nature & Science for just under six years. In fact, I have only been in the field now for just over six years. Before that, I spent my days crunching national child abuse and neglect data. Before that, I was advocating for social justice and victims' rights. And my graduate work? Forensic and investigative psychology. Not even a little bit museum-related. I didn't grow up with dreams of working in a museum. In fact, I rarely walked through the doors of any cultural institution before I turned 30. And now?

Well, you'd be hard-pressed to get me to work anywhere else. I even got a museum-inspired tattoo. Seriously.

Sure, my path is perhaps a bit unusual. But the more I tell the story of how I found my way to museums and hear about the journeys of others, the less unusual it seems. Our field is one in which many roads lead to the same destination. Until the relatively recent growth of museum studies graduate programs, there was no clear path to museum work. Our field lives and breathes Emerson: "Do not go where the path may lead, go instead where there is no path and leave a trail." Many museum greats blazed their own trails and many emerging museum professionals will do the same. Arguably, the more scenic detours, wrong turns, construction, even crashes along the way, the more complete map we will have to visualize and understand the world around us. That depth and breadth of understanding brings what I believe are essential tools in advocating for visitors, audiences and communities. I am much less wary of admitting to museum colleagues how I got here than I am of forgetting where I came from.

As I enter my sixth year in our sector, I recognize the incredible value of what I bring into my work from my "old life." Every day there is something relevant and applicable, from the teen in South London collared for a string of robberies, or the social worker in Washington, DC, who never had enough hours in the day to visit all the foster kids in her caseload. These experiences keep me grounded and help me stay humble; they remind me of what we are and what we aren't. The external lens allows me to keep perspective in a sector that traditionally has been inward-looking and insular.

This isn't a story about why I changed course (though that's a story worth telling, too). Instead, it's a story about how my totally unrelated-to-museums past continues to inform and infuse my work in ways that are essential to my practice and, I believe, are critical to the future of museums and cultural institutions. This is not just my story. Some fellow museum outsiders have helped me reflect on why it's important to acknowledge and embrace the external lens, and how all of us—regardless of how long we've been in this field and even if we've never been in any other—must continue to look from the outside in.

Daryl Fisher of Musynergy Consulting was once a space planner for a large architectural firm, focusing largely on companies and firms that needed office space. "Whatever the case," Daryl remembers, "we began meeting with client representatives at the beginning of the project and continued all the way through completion to determine their needs and ensure that we met them on time and on budget. We called it 'programming' instead of 'evaluation,' but the goals were much the same—ask the right questions in a systematic way to discover the needs of the client/ users." This focus on collaborative and iterative processes has largely influenced her current work in audience research and evaluation. As for lessons learned that have carried over, Daryl cites the importance of gathering feedback from people at all levels. "If we had only talked with the execs, we wouldn't have come up with spaces that functioned well for staff or for the clients they served." Additionally she recognizes "the need to pay as much attention to responses that deviate from the norm as those that support your expectations. One person who saw things differently could make a suggestion that improved the efficiency of an entire organization. By really listening, we'd sometimes pick up on a seemingly random comment that made the difference between a good design and a great design." In the architecture world, it was accepted that programming was a necessity and that good design couldn't happen in a vacuum. "For many years," Daryl observes, "museums based their designs on expert knowledge and constructs, which makes me think that in some ways museums have come late to the notion of getting feedback from our visitors. And it makes me wonder, how might the paradigm shift if we thought of those we serve as clients instead of visitors or audiences?"

Beck Tench, director for innovation and digital engagement at the Museum of Life and Science in Durham, North Carolina, came from the world of graphic design, Web and information architecture. She has held onto that "passionate community of geeks," and feels it is essential to "stay connected to our legacy communities"—for example, bringing museum colleagues into spaces and events created for (in her case) Web geeks, designers and programmers. Beck understands that museums don't necessarily have universal appeal and that "science and art are intimidating and also a foreign language." To keep from losing her outsider's perspective, she says "anytime I realize that I'm pretending to know what's going on, I take a step back and check myself and my assumptions." Beck emphasized the importance of practicing creativity and reflection in our work. "That creative time," she says, "helps me understand where I'm making assumptions, and gives me strategies for fighting them."

Cheryl Kessler, audience researcher and evaluator and founder of Blue Scarf Consulting, worked in industries as disparate as health care, advertising, real estate and law before finding her way to libraries and museums—and then evaluation. "All of my 'old life' jobs," Cheryl says, "revolved around organization, follow-through, being a self-starter *and* a team player, diplomacy *and* tact." She says those skills are the foundation of her work now, "from crafting a proposal, planning evaluation with clients, scheduling data collection, getting data entered, analysis, interpretation or reporting." To keep from losing the outside perspective, Cheryl believes that what she learned about follow-through keeps her "external lens...clear and open." As an external evaluator, Cheryl knows "it's important, even essential, to be objective and continually following up on ideas, comments and questions" to keep from simply doing what's always been done. "There isn't much new under the sun, though there are likely new applications for older routines."

Lisa Sindorf, who works on visitor research and evaluation at the Exploratorium, tutored English Language Learners and scored language exams for international students. She then taught English at a public middle school in Oakland. After four years, she "knew that teaching wasn't a sustainable long-term career path" for her and started thinking about other avenues where she might apply her background and experience. Lisa still employs the methods she learned and used while studying linguistics (interviewing people, transcribing audio, analyzing speech from audio and video recordings). From teaching, she feels she holds onto "a perspective on how kids learn and the mental models they might form about what learning is and how it happens." Working with language learners, Lisa observed that writing that seems clear to a native speaker might cause confusion to a non-native speaker. "That holds true for museum labels as much as for novels," she says. Teaching helped Lisa "better understand the kinds of experiences and prior knowledge kids in Oakland might bring with them when they come to a museum setting." Lisa has stayed in touch with her teacher colleagues and also says she keeps perspective and finds inspiration in attending non-museum conferences, particularly those that focus on a mix of in-school and at-home learning.

Kat Sikes, a recent museum studies graduate student, reminded me that "there is a new and upcoming crop of professionals in the field being shaped by the fruits of earlier labors." In particular, Kat says, "as time keeps moving, kids that participated in the interactive exhibit boom of the late '80s–early '90s (such as myself) are coming into the field." She continues, "In some ways it's strange *not* being an outsider, because from museum professionals I've met, I think the norm has been to be transplants." Kat is a self-described insider, "born into museums, growing up actively as a visitor, and transitioning into a volunteer and professional." Her inside track has had a profound effect on the way she views museums from multiple perspectives. With, and perhaps because of, her true internal lens, Kat has a keen appreciation for outsider points of view. "Former teachers bring invaluable insight into collaboration with the schools. Former theater designers can breathe life into an exhibit that might otherwise get bogged down in a checklist of museum standards for an exhibit. This multidisci-plinary nature of museums comes in handy, as it seems that someone from virtually any background can contribute to them."

All of us, regardless of how or when or why, who fell deeply in love with the mission and work of museums and cultural institutions can continue to go where there is no path, trail-blazing with our unique perspectives, past experiences and personal vantage points. Just as there is no one way to get here, there is no one way to get to where we want to go. Your journey, and all its twists and turns, will add value. Embrace multiplicity; listen to disparate voices; see how diverse experiences can expose us to an entirely new light. Instead of the narrow focus of how to bring the outside in, reflect on ways you can bring yourself out.

Chapter 4

It's Normal to Ask: What Am I Doing Here?

Katarina Ivanišin Kardum

Museum Educator
Technical Museum, Zagreb

F or me, the worlds of science and art have always inter-
twined. During my master's degree studies at the Royal
College of Art in London, I spent a lot of time in the
neighboring natural history and science museums, trying to
find the input for my art work. Subsequently, while teaching
art in London, I encouraged my students to do their research
in museums whenever applicable. In my own artistic work, the
natural history collections remained an inspiration. When I
returned to my native city, I decided to volunteer as a museum
educator in the Dubrovnik Natural History Museum that
was just about to reopen. At the time, the only other staff
member was the director of the museum, a trained biologist.
She saw the potential in my professional background and we
instantly "clicked."

The museum was founded in 1872 and run ever since by great enthusi-
asts and philanthropists. However, for almost three decades it was closed
while an adequate space for the collections was sought. Finally, it reopened

to the public in 2009 in new premises in the old city center. Since the museum had been closed for so long, the local community had lost the memory of it, and there was a need to reanimate their interest. I was not convinced that I was capable of following in the footsteps of these early educators by conducting programs that could foster cultural progress in a small, well-known and yet remote place such as the city of Dubrovnik. I wondered, "What am I doing here?"

At times I felt insecure working in a scientific environment, seemingly totally detached from the scope of my profession. But I decided to focus on those aspects that immediately triggered my curiosity and in which I saw the expanding potential, in terms of both the educational programs and the community involvement. The more involved and familiar I was with the matter, the more certain I was when it came down to delivery. After a year of full-time voluntary work, I decided to take on a permanent position as a museum educator there.

Now, after almost five years, I have devised several educational programs, co-authored the first educational publication (*Protected Species*) for the youngest museum visitors, and the museum's first (didactic) exhibition, even managing to get the backing of the Ministry of Culture. The line connecting all these projects was the interdisciplinary approach, the collaborative work, the blurring of the boundaries between nature and culture, science and art, and, most of all, the playful "artistic" approach to serious, "scientific" issues. The very restricted budget for the programs, although at times frustrating, boosted my own creativity and the creativity of my associates. Most important, the museum's educational programs have contributed to the popularization of both the institution and the field of natural history.

Currently, the museum does not have a permanent exhibition. The collections on exhibit are largely preparations made at the turn of the 20th century, and are a record of the biodiversity of the Dubrovnik region at the time. So with an objective to provoke interest in the local community about this valuable collection, the director and I agreed that we needed to tell a story about the objects.

We started with two curious natural objects from the collection: the head and the caudal fin of an enormous tuna (*Thunnus thynnus*) caught in the vicinity of Dubrovnik in 1897. Looking at those objects in the flesh, one can guess the size of the fish, but the rest of the body is missing. Precisely that missing part became the core of the story we decided to tell by setting up an exhibition titled "How Big Was the Tuna in Our Museum?" Two years of scientific research preceded the exhibition. In parallel, workshops were held with the aim of translating scientific facts into actual forms. Participants were high school students whose contribution was essential in the exhibition set-up and in popularizing the museum and natural history, generally. Working towards the exhibition, we used art techniques to reconstruct the dimensions, estimated on the basis of morphometric characteristics of the tuna. The first step in the process was drawing. This approach and method would have been very common to a scientist 100 years ago. The drawings on the scale of 1:10, and the drawing on the scale of 1:1, were later included in the set-up of the exhibition, illustrating for the visitors how scientific data were given a physical shape. A more complex step was to turn the 2D depiction into a 3D model. A simple and inexpensive way was to make models on the scale of 1:10 by recycling cardboard boxes. In the exhibition display, more than 50 of these models, hanging from the ceiling, illustrated tuna swimming in schools. The 1:1 model was made in collaboration with a 3D modeling studio and a small shipbuilding factory. In the exhibition space it was installed next to the original museum objects, giving a direct answer to the question, "How Big Was the Tuna in Our Museum?" Finally, to reconstruct the way this fish moves, an animation was made using the drawings and the models from the workshops.

When the exhibition opened on International Museum Day in May 2011, it was attended by a large audience from Dubrovnik. This was a result of workshops with children held since 2009, which were regularly reported on by the local media and, on several occasions, by national television. The title of an article published the day after the opening read: "They know how to attract citizens, and children in particular."

Following this successful example from practice, I was reassured that art or art techniques can well complement science. I wondered less often,

"What am I doing here?" However, precisely because of my professional background, I remain aware that in the context of my current job, science should come first and I should say no to those situations, however tempting, that put science in the service of art. Recently, we published the first museum catalogue, *Protected Species,* for which I did eight drawings of museum objects. It is a didactic catalogue, primarily aimed at 5- to 10-year-olds. The drawings give the information about the species' anatomy, while detachable stencils matching the outline of the drawings function as tools that enable the user to animate and manipulate the exhibits in ways that are physically impossible with genuine objects. To promote this publication, I co-authored an animation that does precisely what is described above. By using the detachable stencils, the animation portrays how old museum objects can be brought back to life, while at the same time answering the question often asked by the youngest visitors: "Were these really ever alive?" I believe this is how the museum fulfills its educational potential.

On seeing the animation, a primary school biology teacher asked me to set up an animation class that would complement her biology lessons. My initial thought was to accept the offer because I would enjoy teaching the pupils basic animation skills. However, taking the time to think it over, I realized that I would have to refuse. What I was asked to do was solely to bring my art skills to somebody else's teaching subject, even though the subject in question is indeed very much related to natural history.

I save this approach for my art practice, which parallels my museum job. In my latest work, I use the objective photographs of old dioramas from the collection of the Dubrovnik Natural History Museum. These were made for scientific documentation, to explore the *unnatural* nature of landscape. But that must remain a topic for another conversation.

Chapter 5

Tap into Your Passion

Marjorie Schwarzer

Administrative Director, Museum Studies, University of San Francisco

I will now step over the soft velvet rope
and walk directly into this massive Hudson River
painting and pick my way along the Palisades
with a stick I have snapped off a dead tree.

I will skirt the smoky, nestled towns
and seek the path that leads always outward
until I become lost, without a hope
of ever finding the way back to the museum.
    —Billy Collins, "The Brooklyn Museum of Art"

Museums are places where, as the poet Billy Collins says, we lose ourselves and, in a sense, find ourselves. Let me share with you how I have lost and found myself in museums and what museums mean to me personally. It is this passion, formed very early in my life, that drives my day-to-day professional life.

Whenever I get a new office, cubicle or work space, one of the first things I do to claim my space is hang up a small crumpled print of Paul Gauguin's late-19th-century painting, *Still Life with Three Puppies*. Atop the composition of apples, pears and goblets, three puppies of uncertain breed drink from a large, black, cast-iron pot of water. I have held onto this print since 1963, and it has graced many walls. The original oil painting hangs in the Museum of Modern Art in New York City. My small crumpled copy is also special. It was purchased for me as a gift on the occasion of my first museum visit. On the back is a handwritten inscription in my grand-mother's shaky handwriting and a seal from the place it was purchased: the gift shop at the Albright-Knox Art Museum in Buffalo, New York.

My grandparents bought me the print on my sixth birthday. At my mother's suggestion, my family visited the museum that day to see an exhibition of Pop Art. I remember high concrete walls, large airy spaces and a lot of tall people. Perhaps because the grown-ups got so immersed in the art, I got separated from them. I hardly noticed that I was lost in the museum. I was entranced by the enormous paintings and sculptures. I still remember seeing a cartoonish painting by Roy Lichtenstein. And there was another sculpture in the middle of a gallery made completely out of mir-rors. I crawled inside of it and marveled at how it reflected my body and the surrounding art. My family later found me at the gift shop, staring intently at the print of the puppies.

When I was a teenager, my aunt took me to see my first blockbuster exhibition: the famous King Tut show of 1974. I caught blockbuster fever. I stood in line to see them all: King Tut. Treasures from Germany, from China, from India. I think I was drawn to museums because they offered a profound experience that was within bounds. They awed me, but they did not scare me. I felt safe enough inside of them to lose myself. Unlike the city outside, the museum was a secure place. I was encouraged by my parents, teachers and elders to visit them. After all, they were educational. Yet to me, they were more than just sanctioned educational spaces. For a middle-class kid growing up in a non-religious family, they were my touch point, my sacred ground. I went on to study art history at Washington University in St. Louis. There, when I was 18, I met my future husband. Our first date was to the Saint Louis Art Museum. To this day, whenever Mitchell and I visit museums together—which is often—we have profound conversations (and arguments!) about so many aspects of life. As the years have passed, I have had the pleasure of visiting hundreds, if not thousands, of museums. A few experiences stand out and inform my practice as a museum professional.

Since 1981, I have had the honor to work in museums—as an administrator, an educator, a curator, a writer, a researcher—and to teach future museum professionals about them. The field has changed dramatically, and it is often difficult to make sense of the changes. So many museum professionals think they are alone—that they are the only ones struggling to create that perfect educational program, deal with an exhibition that keeps breaking down, understand audiences, advertise programs, manage budgets and time schedules, cope with a difficult or egotistical employee or staff member, attend to an especially demanding visitor or boss, worry about a collections object that seems to have no paperwork or documentation. In truth, museum professionals—and museums, for that matter—would not exist without each other. And they would not exist without a vast array of other institutions—worldwide cultural movements, universities, national and local governments, educational and legal systems, businesses, media outlets, auction houses, the Internet, the global economy, charitable foundations. After all, that's why museums exist. We aren't isolated entities. We are places like the sculpture I saw so many years ago at the Albright Knox Museum that reflect our image back to us, in multiple dimensions.

Art museums show us works of stunning and timeless beauty as well as contemporary artworks that mix up media and color, and stimulate our senses. But do they stretch our creativity far enough? Science museums impart romantic ideas about the battle of man and the natural world, as well as contemporary ideas about exploration and discovery. But what about the role of ethics and religious belief systems? History museums transport us to the past so we can make sense of our world today; they also awe us with the sheer volume of production of societies past. But whose history? And what kinds of identities do they help to forge? Zoos put us face-to-face with exotic living creatures; botanical gardens soothe and nourish us and remind us of the world's diversity. But do we have a right to collect living things? Children's museums give us room to celebrate and interact with people from different backgrounds. They teach us that object-based learning is fun, especially when we learn together. But do they serve parents and adults well?

The answers lie in the fact that museums are filled with bright and motivated people: visitors, staff, volunteers and trustees who have the passion to engage in these questions. We need to honor them, treat them well and help them to help museums flourish. For, despite all of the challenges, where would our society be if there were no place to visit treasures, contemplate art and history, experience scientific and natural phenomena at our own pace, with those whom we love and admire? If there were no place that preserved our history or our creative process? If there were no place free to educate in a way that meets people's needs as opposed to the requirements of a school system or testing agency? If in a world of so many different religions, points of view and life journeys, there were no centralized secular place that allowed for spiritual contemplation? If in a restless contemporary world, characterized by mobility, immigration and technological speed, there were no sites for reflection, tranquility and stillness? If in a global economy, driven by material acquisition, there were no sites for preservation and regeneration? These are the questions and passions that move me when I think about museums.

I know you have your own set of questions and passions. What I encourage you to do is to tap into them and take the time to lose yourself in the museum.

Afterword

K. Tierney Sneeringer

Luce Foundation Center Program Specialist
Smithsonian American Art Museum

I did not know that I wanted to climb the ladder when I started my first museum job. I had always wanted to do my best, try new things and be successful, but I would never have used the word ambitious to describe myself. It also never dawned on me during my first few months in the museum that I might not be prepared—I said yes to everything! And if I was not saying yes, I was pursuing new projects and ways to develop my role in the museum. Luckily my boss was incredibly supportive of my experiments: sometimes they were successful, other times they were not.

Saying yes, taking risks and finding value in all experiences are key elements to being a successful educator and museum professional. Leah Melber reinforces the importance of this in the first chapter of this book. Her philosophy of saying yes and figuring it out later could not be more apt, especially for us emerging professionals. I am not sure if knowing this would have calmed my nerves when I first started at the museum, but it certainly does now as I pursue more complex, perhaps "out there" projects. She also noted that taking risks sometimes means failing and learning from those experiences, something that resonated with me, as the idea of reflective practice was a large part of my graduate studies.

While completing my master's degree prepared me for many things, I am not sure I was mentally prepared for how competitive it was to get a job. Reading Brad Irwin's chapter on making the most of a job opportunity reminded me that my current position, as originally posted, was not ideal, as it was part-time. I applied anyway because it seemed like an amazing opportunity and I was ready to put my passion for art and museums to work. Kathleen Tinworth also shared this passion, but unlike me, she changed fields in mid-career to work in a museum. She cites other examples of professionals who made the leap and describes how they have benefited by using this idea of reflective practice and finding value in every experience, a.k.a. the "outside lens," in her words. Both Tinworth's and Irwin's chapters show us that if we are well prepared and determined, we can utilize our skills anywhere.

It is important to note, however, that having the right skill sets and knowledge is not always enough. Melber's mental checklist in Chapter 1 reminds us that we need to make sure we also have support from other colleagues in the field and the desire to grow professionally. All of these things allowed Irwin, Tinworth and Chapter 4 author Katarina Ivanišin Kardum to be successful while switching fields and specialties. Professional relationships and "museum friends," as Irwin calls them, are crucial when trying to find your footing in the field.

Networking is sometimes given a bad rap. It is only in the past few years that I have realized how critical it is (this is also around the time I openly started referring to myself as ambitious). My turning point was in September 2011 when I attended an international conference alone. Tired of awkwardly sitting silent while everyone around me chatted, I turned to the person next to me and started a conversation. Putting myself out there helped me meet colleagues from across the globe and, strangely enough, boosted my confidence as a museum professional. I have since found that these relationships can provide you with a wealth of wisdom and great advice, such as was given Irwin early in his career, and allow you to work collaboratively in and outside your museum, like Kardum. People will be happy to help you grow and introduce you to other colleagues, and will take pride in your future success. In fact, my participation in this book can be traced back to conversations at that international conference.

This section in the book also reminds us that we should not over-plan what those future successes might be. This is hard! And yet, this is exactly what can get us in over our heads (remember Melber's checklist) or lead us to unexpected opportunities, as it did for all of the authors in this section. Per their experiences, it seems that being flexible and open are qualities needed to climb the ladder. I would also add being lifetime learners to this list; all of the authors in this section mentioned adding skills to their repertoire. Oh, and passion—a quality that I am sure all of us possess.

Things to Ponder:

Have you ever said yes to an opportunity without thinking? What were the outcomes of the situation? What were you able to take away from it?

1. How might you better learn from your successes and mistakes?

2. How can you find value in a past, perhaps unrelated professional experience and incorporate it into your current position?

3. How can you meet more people in your field or community who share the same professional values?

4. What can you do on your own to continue to grow as a museum professional?

Section 2: Doing Your Best

Chapter 6

Don't Just Color Outside the Lines—
Imagine and Draw Your Own Picture

Lynn McRainey

Chief Education Officer and Elizabeth F. Cheney Director of Education
Chicago History Museum

O n my first visit to Chicago, my friends and I arrived late at night. With the city's distinctive skyline a distant silhouette, I had to delay my introduction to Chicago until the next morning, when friends and I boarded a southbound Ravenswood train (now the Brown Line). My ears immediately filled with the rattling and screeching of the train as it rumbled down the tracks. My hands grasped the metal pole for balance on the curves, and my body was swept into a rhythmic motion mirroring the train's swinging and swaying movements. Inside the car, my eyes studied the faded map of the route, trying to orient myself as each station was announced. Outside I viewed the unfamiliar landscape whisking by as it morphed from low neighborhood rooftops to the towering skyscrapers. And as other passengers crowded around me, I was no longer a first-time tourist, but a Chicagoan riding the L.

While this experience holds personal significance, the L ride also has meaning for me professionally in illustrating the evolution of my understanding of learning and my appreciation for how and where it occurs. Although my formal education was in American studies and art history, my career as a museum educator has been an independent study on the meaning of learning. Over the years, colleagues have been guest instructors teaching me valuable lessons through their mentoring and conversations about the role of education in museums. My own teaching style developed as I observed skilled educators modeling best practices.

My studies have also been shaped by an extended course syllabus found in the books and journals that populate my office bookshelves. Unknown to the outside observer (or borrower), I have designated a shelf close to my desk for a collection that I turn to time and again. These books share a similar look, with their worn covers held together with tape, and dogeared pages colored with yellow highlights and scribbles in the margins. On first glance, the eclectic list of titles such as *Releasing the Imagination, Eavesdropping: A Life by Ear,* and *Children's Minds, Talking Rabbits, and Clockwork Oranges* may seem irrelevant to my studies in museum education. But these are the books I turn to when I need to refuel and reaffirm my practice, fine-tune my definition of learning or be inspired to think differently.

It is through one author's writings in particular that I have come to understand a tool that I, as a lifelong learner, personally value and that I draw on professionally—the imagination. Kieran Egan, professor at Canada's Simon Fraser University and founder of the Imaginative Education Research Group (ierg.net), has written extensively on the critical role the imagination plays in learning. Imaginative Education engages the learner affectively through cognitive tools that we all use to make sense of the world. Without realizing it at the time, my imagination was fully engaged on that first L ride as I used my own personal tool-kit to construct meaning about a new place and experience: my senses (hands, ears and eyes), rhythms (body mirroring the train's movements), graphic organizers (matching station names to map), extremes and limits of reality (comparing building heights) and role play (pretending to be a Chicagoan). Drawing on the same tools—the senses, graphic organizers, extremes/limits and role play—a teacher can plan lessons and a museum educator can design experiences to engage students and visitors affectively with any subject or topic.

Over the past 10 years, I have continued to turn to the writings of Kieran Egan and the IERG website to shape the design of interpretive products and experiences. Outcomes such as flexible thinking and affective engagement continue to illustrate for me what learning should look like in a museum. As I assumed a leadership role for institutional planning and special projects, the imagination and the cognitive tools of Imaginative Education took on a new meaning and purpose for me as I turned to them not only for the design of interpretive experiences, but also for shaping the process for their development. When wearing my project-manager hat, I have discovered that the imagination offers options for exploring uncharted territories in its ability to transport the process, the team and myself beyond the known. The imagination has the ability to stimulate flexible thinking and affective engagement not only in museum visitors but also in the museum staff who create these experiences.

For Imaginative Education, routine is the enemy of the imagination. But for me, routine is both enemy and ally. My work as department head has focused on managing resources of staff, time and money as the next project, program or collaboration is launched. Guised as "the tried and true" approach, routine becomes an ally in its ability to get the job done and check another item off an ever expanding to-do list. As enemy, routine's prescriptive nature denies any team the opportunity to be engaged and experiment with alternate possibilities for advancing familiar tasks or new projects.

To avoid a complacent practice of routine, I try to keep close at hand two cognitive tools of imaginative education—"a sense of wonder" and "change of context"—as a means of re-engaging myself with my work and opening the door to flexible thinking among team members. Competing meeting schedules and multiple project teams can render these tools ineffective. But when integrated into a process, I am able to clear my mind of the routines driven by institutional policies and culture, and consider alternate possibilities for how I approach my work as both team leader and team member.

The "sense of wonder" allows me to reconnect and re-engage with the familiar aspects of work. This device allows us to approach any topic with eyes (and minds) to discover and embrace what makes it special and unique. By bringing a sense of wonder to a program, a children's gallery or guided tours, I was able to take a fresh look at the opportunities each might hold. The trick is to be willing to ask "what if?" for each of these programs, and to be open to exploring the merits of what the answers might reveal. Personally the "what if?" moments have taken me in a range of unexpected directions. What if adult programs were not dependent on the changing themes of temporary exhibitions? What if children used their senses to interpret history? What if there were no guided tours for school groups? What if an audio tour was not narrated? It is the projects that were born of "what if" moments that have sparked a renewed passion for what is possible, bringing unexpected opportunities for myself, the team and the museum visitor.

While museums pride themselves on being alternative classrooms that offer new approaches and experiences for exploring a range of disciplines, limited time is spent discussing or considering the environment and culture in which these products are created. Project teams' "classrooms" are the conference rooms that become overcrowded with competing schedules, departmental silos, personal agendas and apathy. It is amazing how a new space can generate fresh ideas and alternative directions. A simple change of context led to new discoveries for a school programs team exploring the possibilities of moving away from guided tours for student groups, and for an exhibition team reinterpreting one of the first elevated trains in Chicago. For the former, the team walked two blocks to our neighbor, The Second City, to take two afternoon workshops on "Improvisation for Creative Pedagogy." For the latter, the exhibit team traded the museum conference room for a moving L train. For both, I had to ignore the voice of routine that said these alternate approaches would take up too much time, with no certainty of the outcomes. But the imagination thrives in new environments. The rewards for changing the context were immeasurable for both teams. For the school programs team, staff participated in theater games and discovered first-hand the merits of an experience-based approach to learning. For the exhibit team, a three-hour meeting on a moving L train produced a healthy list of sensory impressions that continued to inform the exhibit process.

To allow the imagination to flourish in your work, you need to create an environment and culture that will welcome and nurture its presence. Through my own experiences, I have identified three mindsets that allow imagination to take the lead over routine: experimentation, openness to uncertainty and persistence.

Be Willing to Experiment

The possibilities that come from engaging a team's imagination require a culture that is willing to experiment, test and draw conclusions—the same activities we invite our visitors to perform. But with experimentation also comes the possibility of failure. Six activity stations became the school programs team's answer to "What if there were no guided tours?" While summative evaluation and nine months of use confirmed that four of the initial six were successfully engaging students, two had to be reworked and tested, resulting in a total overhaul of one cart and the retirement of another.

Be Open to Uncertainty

The imagination is not always crystal clear about the details of an effectively managed project. Uncharted territories sometimes require a leap of faith among team members. When creating a children's gallery, the curator and I chose to keep the process open to avoid defining too soon the thematic focus of the exhibition. Instead we allowed conversations with our target audiences of 8- and 9-year-olds to inform the team's discussions and exploration of a range of interpretive approaches. We were 15 months into the project before we were confident that the senses would offer our audience both cognitive and physical access to the past.

Be Persistent

The imagination is not always a welcome or trusted addition to the team process. "We have never done it that way, it will take too much time, if it is not broken why fix it, and you are being too ambitious" are all phrases that can stop you and your imagination in your tracks. I have learned to try to listen and discover what lies at the heart of these statements in order to navigate the process around attitudes that may threaten the time needed for a good idea to develop into an out-of-the-box approach.

Whether I am wearing the hat of department head, project director or team member, the cognitive tools of Imaginative Education infuse wonder and passion into my work. Just as we strive to engage our visitors in those "ah-ha" defining moments, it is equally important to identify and plan a process to fuel our own imaginations. A sense of wonder and change of context led me to new discoveries and unexpected possibilities. My friends still talk about that transformative L ride on my first visit to Chicago. While I cannot remember what museum exhibition we attended that day (the motivation for the weekend trip), I still hold that ride vividly in my memory. I was affectively engaged with the moment, and my imagination began to consider the possibilities. Less than a year later, I was asking myself, "What if I took a nine months' position in Chicago?" Twenty-plus years later, I call myself a Chicagoan and I still think the L is the best ride in town.

Chapter 7

Speak the Local Language

William B. Crow

Managing Museum Educator
Metropolitan Museum of Art

Within the first hour of arriving in Spain for my junior year abroad, I managed to lose the directions to the local bus station and break my glasses. Two of the four wheels on my brand-new American Tourister luggage wobbled away in opposite directions. I must have appeared as discombobulated as I felt, since a teenager approached me and offered to help. I can clearly remember her sympathetic expression and how grateful I was that someone came to my aid. Although I could comprehend a few words in her sentences, her use of informal phrases and slang made it impossible for me to completely understand what she was saying. I couldn't piece together all of the new words and phrases she was using to make any meaning.

I gathered myself, and after a four-hour bus ride I finally arrived at the Universidad de Salamanca. I climbed the steps of the 700-year-old main building and located the office of my new faculty advisor, the chair of the literature department. He greeted me warmly, but then spoke the most

formal and erudite Castillian Spanish I had ever heard. I stared blankly
at him and somehow mustered a response. His vocabulary and sentence
structure had almost no relationship to the Spanish I had learned from my
high school teacher from Cuba. Hadn't I been a good student in my Spanish
classes? I could recite all of the rules of the subjunctive, and was a pro at
knowing when to use *"por"* instead of *"para."* In my first 24 hours in Spain, I
struggled to navigate the different modalities of expression.

In my daily practice as a museum educator, I am often reminded of
those first few moments in Spain. I don't mean that in my work at the
Metropolitan I have to immerse myself in Spanish, Japanese or French, as
much as our former director and polyglot, Philippe de Montebello, might
have welcomed this. But at any given time I find that I have to adjust my
own communication modes in order to respond to the unique roles and
values of my colleagues and museum visitors.

If you've ever embarked on learning a new language, you'll recognize the
learning curve. Beginner language classes are filled with some basic primers:
learning what Marisol is going to *comprar* at the *supermercado;* hearing Jean-
Luc prepare for a *fête* with his friends on *la rue Claire*. It's not very difficult
to memorize some new vocabulary, or to mimic the phrases that the audio
track plays (usually involving some very animated friends who are shopping
for cheese or deciding on a birthday present). Once you have that foundation of vocabulary, grammar rules, verb tenses and common expressions,
it's possible to get by. The harder part begins when you find that you need
to make choices based on the situation and the participants. Will you use
a more formal tense and vocabulary when speaking to a friend's parent?
When is it okay to use slang? Do some words shift in meaning, based on
the location or culture where they are used?

Museums, like many organizations, have their own institutional culture,
and so the language that is used within the museum is often unique. When
I began working at the Met, my first experience with this "culture shock"
was simply finding my way around the building. I would receive an e-mail
with directions to a meeting that read "From Wing K take LAW Spine Elev
to Roof (exit east side doors) by Security and past Fairchild Conservation
to Kravis Conf Room." Over the years, I learned more of the local lingo: the

"sweep" is the term security uses for the process of closing the building to visitors; "Watsonline" is the cataloguing system for the museum's libraries; we often say Met Museum in a conversation with an outside stakeholder to distinguish us from the Metropolitan Opera.

But as all educators know, effective communication isn't about memorizing specialized terms—it's about deep listening. Part of becoming a deep listener is to know your audience. What is that person's role in the museum? What might she need or value in order to do her job? Given the situation at hand, how is this person likely to react to my request? A few years ago when I had the opportunity to participate in a leadership institute at the Getty, a wonderful educator from Stanford Business School, David Bradford, spoke of the need to "exchange common currencies." Like speaking a language, it's critical to communicate with an understanding of what each party values or needs in order to make progress or achieve a common goal.

I'm not always successful at this "currency exchange." A few years ago, when we were exploring the use of online technologies to create a professional development program for teachers, I called a meeting with several members of our IT staff. I remember starting the meeting by telling these computer specialists about all of the exciting possibilities this new program format could offer—participants could exchange information and resources, they could embed digital images from the museum's website directly into their online lessons and they could create their own "e-portfolios." Just as I thought I was sealing the deal by proclaiming that all of this could be hosted on a server outside the museum, I was stopped dead in my tracks. "How are these digital assets managed after the program?" one asked. Another asked, "How do you plan to support this program, given that our IT staff is already oversubscribed?" And the one that I thought would surely be the death knell, "Are you proposing that our own museum content is going to live on a server outside the institution?"

Sitting in that conference room in the midst of all of those questions made me realize that I wasn't speaking the local language. In my enthusiasm for what the technology could offer to support this program, I wasn't speaking to the concerns of the IT staff. They were understandably preoccupied with issues around digital resource management, sustainability and licensing. Over a period of months, with additional meetings based in the target language (i.e., addressing these concerns), the program moved forward with the support and endorsement of the IT staff.

Unfortunately, learning how to speak, listen or "exchange currencies" effectively in your museum doesn't come with vocabulary lists or funny cartoons like most language textbooks. But, as a former high school Spanish teacher myself, I can tell you that a key to learning effective communication is to practice, practice, practice. So in this spirit, I offer a few exercises. For each scenario, consider how you might phrase your request or statement as if you were speaking to someone in your own institution.

Instructions: Adapt the following in accordance with the individual's role and context. Imagine you were speaking to:

A Busy Development Officer

You want to say:	I need money to support the programs I oversee.
But you might say:	_____ .
Try saying this:	I noticed recently that the Jones Foundation is starting to fund education programs that are similar to ours. When I went on their website, I saw that their application requirements are very straightforward, with deadlines that would give us plenty of time to prepare a strong proposal.

A Curator Preparing for a Scholarly Exhibition

You want to say:	What use is an exhibition if no one from the general public can benefit from it?
But you might say:	_____ .
Try saying this:	This sounds like a landmark exhibition that will break new ground. I'd like to learn more about it so that we can find the strongest possible connections for all of our museum visitors.

A Stressed-Out School Principal

You want to say: The value and magic of being in the museum goes way beyond formal learning, so you should forget about all of that standardized testing stuff and just tell your students to get here as quickly as possible.

But you might say: _____.

Try saying this: We'd be excited to welcome your faculty at the museum for a professional development workshop. The skills and subjects that the museum can support are very broad, so we can help your teachers accomplish their goals, while also helping students see that learning can happen outside of school.

A Teenager Thinking About Signing Up for a Drawing Class

You want to say: Developing your artistic skills, building a portfolio for college, and meeting creative people can have an incredible impact in your life and career.

But you might say: _____ .

Try saying this: Are you into drawing? This is going to be an awesome class.

As this exercise may have revealed, gaining fluency in the local languages that are spoken by your colleagues and visitors isn't as simple as completing a worksheet. It's different from the language drills and exams we completed back in high school or college. It's a skill that isn't about memorizing the jargon of a specific group or profession. Nor is it about providing lip service, altering your message to only what an individual wants to hear or kowtowing to the establishment.

What you'll find, with lots of practice, is that speaking the local language is about understanding people and their needs. Listening closely, paying attention to the situation at hand and tailoring your communication can open the door for opportunities, and can help others understand you.

Chapter 8

You Work for the People, Not the Institution

Beverly Serrell

Director

Serrell & Associates

When I got fired from my job as curator of education at Shedd Aquarium, my mother was devastated. She had been so proud of me for working at such a famous place, and she told all her friends—and anybody else who'd listen—that I had a wonderful position of responsibility, and a big department and so on.

In fact, I, too, had always been proud to say that I worked for the largest inland aquarium in the world. I hadn't been especially interested in fish when I started there in 1970, but I was totally enthusiastic about the idea of teaching people about biology and ecology with a living collection in a beautiful, iconic institution on Chicago's lakefront. In the eight years that I worked there, the education facilities grew from a tiny office in a room once called "the gravel bin" to a new multiple-service space, the Aquatic Science Center, with classrooms, two wet labs, a library, lunchroom and lovely offices for my expanded staff. I loved my job.

Well, actually, I loved my job at Shedd for about six of those eight years, when my trajectory of growth and learning was on a steep upward curve. I had expanded the education department to what seemed then like its limits, and I was ready to take on bigger fish, so to speak. Not the director's job, but the exhibits department and the reinterpretation of the aquatic displays upstairs in the main galleries. I knew what the institution needed!

Getting fired did not come as a complete surprise and, in retrospect, I could see it coming. I didn't listen to and respond to the needs of my director. I was known as "cheeky and presumptuous." I made the mistake of not taking direction from my supervisor. Instead, I operated like a free agent, making my own decisions about what was in the best interests of the institution. I challenged my boss in front of other staff members during meetings. I didn't realize that if I had a difference of opinion, he would be more receptive in a private, one-on-one discussion. I learned this after I left, by reflecting on how other female staff members dealt with disagreements successfully.

I've seen other people get fired, laid off or let go from museums they loved. They really cared about the place, they were loyal, so how could this happen? Because the relationship was personal, even familial, they often harbor long-term resentment. I was fortunate in that my boss and I had a healing conversation after I left, and several years later I was hired by Shedd as a consultant to do some of the exhibition-related work I'd always wanted to do.

There is more letting go now that museum budgets are so tight. Maybe it *is* the institution that is firing people now. Maybe it's not so personal.

Leaving a job abruptly and not by choice can have its advantages. Sometimes we stick around because of fear of change or the unknown. Getting bumped out forces one to take stock of the situation with new clarity: What do I *really* want to do? Whom do I want to do it with?

On your job search, consider an organization because you admire the people you'll be working with, not because it is a great match between your academic degree and your personal mission for the museum. If you are lucky and select carefully, you will work with people who are on the same page with you, philosophically. This is especially tricky these days, when so many museums use the team approach to developing exhibitions, and the likelihood of everyone's thoughts meshing harmoniously is slim.

It's reasonable to express disagreement and to hash out creative differences with your boss or colleagues, but once you've had your say, you need to know when to stand down. Remind yourself to pick your battles.

Sometimes it can help to put your concerns in writing to make your position absolutely clear and to document that you have raised awareness about a risk (maybe it's a risk to the timeline, or the budget or the quality of a visitor experience). Either you will get attention on an issue or you can put your mind at rest that you've done what you can within the limits of your authority. What you don't want to do is to raise the alarm with others at your boss's level or go over your boss's head, as you will be perceived as a loose cannon, or worse, not a team player.

It can help to recognize that really bad ideas will often die under their own weight, especially if you are in a good organization overall, so don't waste your ammunition.

The comments above deal mainly with a full-time job as a staff member. What if your choices include being a temporary hired hand?

As a consultant, you really do work for the people, not the institution. They contact you and they hire you because they like your skills and ideas. Forty hours of work for a big, famous urban museum represents the same income as 40 hours at a small nature center, but the work might actually mean more to the staff at a small place than to those at the mega-museum.

As a consultant, it can be easier to give the client what they want, even if you don't agree 100 percent. Your identity is not married to the institution's, nor do you have a territory or a department to defend. You can suggest alternate ideas that you value, but it is easier to let go of them when you are an independent agent. Maybe the next client will be more open to them.

You will probably miss the daily contact with a tight-knit group of colleagues if you are a consultant, but you will not miss the petty politics. You will probably work more efficiently and effectively—and get more praise for it because outside talent is often more vocally valued than staff's. There's a lot more risk and uncertainty, but working for the really wonderful people who populate museum staffs is very rewarding. You just don't get to wear the team T-shirt.

Chapter 9

How to Be a Kick-Ass, Not a Kiss-Ass: Learning to Face Conflict and Stand Up for What's Right

Sheri Bernstein

Vice President and Director of Education
Skirball Cultural Center

E ver since I was young, my father has told me I am a people-person, by which he means that I know what to say to connect with others and make them feel good about themselves—and myself. A case in point is my great-aunt Rose whose housedresses I instinctively complimented as a child; she was a big fan of mine. Caring about what others feel and wanting to be liked and appreciated were part of what steered me toward museum education and away from the curatorial realm, where being a people-person seemed to be, at best, tolerated.

The good thing about museum educators who are "people-people" (and I've encountered a number of us in this field over the years) is that we do value others' feelings and opinions—our constituents' and our colleagues.' We are rarely dictatorial and we play well with others in the sandbox. But what I have found in my own case is that being a people-person has at times made me conflict-avoidant, to the detriment of my work. On a number of occasions, I've failed to go to bat for an idea even when I felt it was best for the students, teachers or families our museum served, or for our institution itself, because doing so risked making the people in my immediate professional world—docents, colleagues or (the horror!) my supervisors—unhappy with me.

The first time it really hit home that I might be overly appeasing and not just a really pleasant and easy gal to work with was about seven years ago when I took a Work Behavior Style test administered by a management coach brought in to support our staff. The test involved answering a slew of multiple-choice questions on how we react in different work situations, both when things are going smoothly and when they are not. Our work styles were then typed with respect to the following four behavior categories:

1. Amiable (a person who prioritizes being liked/appreciated and keeping others happy)

2. Expressive (a formulator and champion of new creative ideas)

3. Analyzer (a gatherer of information and master of facts)

4. Driver (a person who takes the reins and gets things done)

My test results showed that when the climate at work was relatively non-stressful, I had strong Amiable and Analyzer qualities, a decent amount of Expressive and a bit of Driver. When tension was high, however, I was so strongly Amiable that barely a trace of any other work style remained. As I mulled over these results, what came to mind were the many times I had made safe choices in order to avoid ruffling feathers, even when I felt sure other decisions would have yielded better outcomes. I realized that I really needed to muster some more moxie and worry less about displeasing someone in the process. Especially when the going got tough and the stakes were high, I had to bust out my inner Expressive and Driver if I was going to be effective at serving our visitors' and the institution's interests—and my own interests as a professional, as well.

Two examples come to mind. The first involves the creation of a brand new, permanent, participatory children's and family destination that opened in 2007 as Noah's Ark at the Skirball. As the project director at the helm of a brilliant but unwieldy creative team, I had to learn to push back against my supervisors' vision of a more Disneyesque, conventional children's space. I knew inside that the latter wasn't the way to go because 1. we could never do the Disney model as well as Disney; 2. it wasn't an appropriate model for us anyway, given our mission and cross-cultural sensibility; and 3. we should seek to create a *new* model that other cultural institutions could build on in the future. The process of pushing back and advocating for what was right gave me daily heartburn, but it paid off. One pivotal moment, when I actually considered leaving the project because the discord was so stressful, involved holding my ground, along with the project manager, in the selection of life-size, black-silhouetted animals as the exhibition's wall graphics (although a marketing consultant warned our supervisors that we'd be crazy to do this; we'd scare the kids, she said, and would be better off with teal and purple animals with smiley faces). Standing up for what our creative team felt was best—and testing it directly with visitors rather than listening to consultant advisors—turned out to be a crucial decision. Not only has Noah's Ark at the Skirball received a number of design awards, but more important, the feedback from visitors has been stellar and has more than made up for the arduous creation process.

The second example involves my rather non-illustrious history of overseeing the docent corps during my early years as the Skirball's head of education. Specifically, I had a track record of appeasing and acquiescing to school-tour docents—letting them dictate the style and even, to a large degree, the content of the programs they facilitated, even though I knew deep down that this wasn't serving our student visitors optimally. What we needed were docents who facilitated discussions rather than delivered information to passive listeners, and docents who met students where they were and framed their interactions around things of inherent interest to the students. But bringing about this change felt overwhelming because I couldn't face upsetting the vocal members of this 60-plus band of school-tour docents (many of whom fit the profile of my Aunt Rose who, as you may remember, always appreciated my compliments). When I finally faced the music and made long-needed changes in the school-tour content and the pedagogical approach—buoyed, in part, by the success of Noah's Ark and the clear payoff of standing up for what I felt was right—the quality of our student-tour experiences improved tremendously. Plus, while a number of docents were fighting mad at first, and a percentage of those folks quit, most of the docents who stayed were ultimately pleased with the changes because they could see their positive impact on student engagement.

Some clarifications are in order at this point. Being kick-ass is not the same as being a pain-in-the-ass—someone who constantly, vociferously and indiscriminately campaigns for her own ideas and never takes "no" for an answer. Whether it's your boss (in which case, you're running the risk of insubordination) or your co-workers whom you're always standing up to and foisting your own ideas upon, doing so won't help you realize your vision, and most likely will do the opposite. You need to know when to stand up and when not to.

Here's what I ask myself when I'm deciding whether to put myself out there with an idea or an approach that might be unpopular:

1. Is the main reason for *not* speaking up that you don't want to ruffle feathers and risk having people upset with you? If YES, proceed to the next question.

2. Is there a chance that you'll be listened to? If YES, proceed to the next question. Don't bother, if not. Save your voice for another situation when you actually have a chance of being heard. Sometimes there are so many factors—generally political ones—stacked against you that it isn't worth trying. And in fact, doing so will ruin your credibility the next time you want to put an idea out there.

3. Do you feel that your idea (or your way of approaching a problem) will significantly help the audiences that your institution serves and/ or your institution itself? Would the other ideas on the table, or leaving things status quo, hinder your institution's efforts to serve its audiences or weaken your institution in some way? These questions, particularly the last one, are sometimes hard to answer. But if your inclination is YES, then leave the comfort of the Amiable quadrant and go for it.

Once you decide to voice and/or stand up for a big idea, you need to find a diplomatic way to do so. Here's where it comes in handy to be an Amiable. Harness your ability to say things in palatable ways and make people feel good about themselves. Here are some general suggestions:

1. Focus on articulating the yield of your idea in terms of your audiences and/or your institution's well-being, and frame your assessment of other ideas in the same way.

2. Downplay that it's your idea and avoid using the personal pronoun as much as you can.

3. Look for the common ground. If there's a thread of similarity between what you're suggesting and what others at the table are saying, affirm their ideas and connect your own to them. Remember that it's not about getting credit; it's about getting the best outcome for your audiences, your museum and the team of folks that you're part of. If things work out well because of what you've advocated, there will be plenty of credit to go around.

I've found that taming my people-pleaser instinct is an ongoing challenge. After being an approval addict for so long, it's easy to slip back into old patterns, as with any addiction, especially during extra-pressured times when supervisors and co-workers are feeling stressed and short-tempered. I've found, though, that the process does get somewhat easier over time as Driver muscles develop and strengthen. And from my perspective, it's a challenge worth taking on. In fact, it's an essential one for all of us "people-people" to undertake if we're truly going to excel as leaders within our own institutions and as members of the larger museum field.

Chapter 10

Volunteering Has Value

Sarah Marcotte

Museum Services: Mars Public Engagement
Jet Propulsion Laboratory

Picture in your mind a pea-sized snowball, perched at the crest of a steep hill. Suddenly this tiny clump of snow begins to roll, picking up more snow as it descends, gaining momentum and speed as it grows larger. Now think of that tiny pea as a recent instance when you were offered an interesting professional opportunity. Could that opportunity be the one that will snowball into larger ones, giving your career momentum and speed?

I remember a winter day in my manager's sun-filled office when she asked me to serve as the webmaster for the Museum Educators of Southern California (MESC), a volunteer group that organizes professional development programs for museum educators. I jumped at the chance, despite the fact that I didn't really know how to work on websites and was still in the emerging phase of my career. My service on that regional board later gave me the confidence to apply to two other museum-related national boards, to which I was accepted. I served on the Communications Committee of the Museum Education Roundtable, which publishes *The Journal of Museum Education*, and as the secretary of the Media & Technology Professional

Network, one of 13 professional interest committees affiliated with the American Alliance of Museums. Now my network of personal and professional contacts stretches across the United States and gives me a wide perspective on our field.

I set that snowball in motion by saying "yes."

Start Local Before Going Global

There are many ways to raise your professional profile, such as conducting original research about visitor learning, or developing innovative revenue-generating programs and exhibits. These endeavors will get you noticed within your institution, but to get your name out there in the wider field you need to tap into local and national conferences. National museum conferences depend on a decentralized network of committees to feed conference content to them. Those committees often draw on the local networks of their members. One easy way to set your snowball in motion would be to find a local museum-related committee, join it and serve meaningfully, then use that experience to gain some traction with the national groups. I am an educator by training, so I found a museum educator organization. However, there are committees related to every aspect of museum operations, from registrars to exhibit designers, to museum security guards. All of them contribute to the programming that happens at conferences and all of them have local networks in every state.

Living as we do in the Age of Google, it is not hard to find local and national groups. But you may have to be a little creative in how you search. Don't be afraid to pick up the phone. I got started in museum education by cold-calling a local museum education department and asking a stranger how she got her job. She had a master's degree in museum education from Bank Street College, which a few years later became my alma mater, too. Call the large urban museums in your state, or call the national organizations and ask how to connect to local chapters. E-mail works, too, but you will be surprised at the results yielded by a simple phone call.

Joining a committee is as easy as finding out when and where the meetings are and showing up. Applying for a board position may require a statement of interest and your C.V. Emphasize your willingness to commit your time and energy and to take on several tasks. Treat this as applying for a job, because if you are successful, committee and board work can lead to better jobs.

Commit, Don't Quit

Now for the reality-check of serving on local and national boards. It takes time, and in some cases, it takes money. Your money. If you are fortunate, your management will support your desire to serve on a committee, as it raises your museum's profile as well. However, not all institutions believe your professional time should be spent on conference calls, sending e-mails and printing flyers to advertise a meeting. In that case, you will be working through your lunch breaks and before and after your already long work day. I spent many nights and weekends hunched over my computer, updating WordPress websites and sending e-newsletters. But in my case, the rewards were many: I can now say I have organized a two-day conference on museum education and technology and coordinated a national museum media competition and awards ceremony. The work was interesting and gave me a macro perspective on the forces driving museum interpretation, use of media devices in exhibitions and trends in education research.

However, on every board there are a few people who join and never do a thing. I do not recommend this approach. Obviously life and work sometimes present challenges that prevent you from fulfilling your obligation. Be proactive if you know this is happening and resign with a polite, apologetic letter. Well-run boards will notice the no-show people and ask them to either start participating or resign. Weaker boards will tolerate the no-shows, creating tension and resentment among the people who are still volunteering their time. If you join a committee and disappear, your reputation will suffer. If you apply to another committee or even for a new job, your tarnished image may speak louder than the list of presentations on your resumé.

What about the money? Many of us work in nonprofit institutions, and our salaries are not in the realm of the Fortune 500. Being asked to take on additional personal expense may not be realistic for you, so keep that in mind. I was required to purchase memberships for each of the organizations I "governed." If you are serving as a board member, this is not a choice. It is assumed that you will contribute resources as a sign that you are truly committed to the financial well-being of the organization. You may also have to pay your own travel expenses to meetings. Some are local, and it's the price of a few gallons of gas. If you serve on national boards, you may be expected to travel to national meetings at your own expense. Again, your museum may support your efforts and use institutional funds for your membership and travel, in addition to approving your time. However, it's unwise to count on this.

What You Can Expect

The three groups I served with organize programs, publish a journal, and coordinate a museum media competition and awards ceremony. Two of the three committees have a national reach, so most of our work is conducted on monthly conference calls, a slew of e-mail and at face-to-face meetings at the American Alliance of Museums Annual Meeting. The work is very similar to what museum educators do weekly, because it is for museum professionals who want to attend programs once in a while instead of coordinating them! Organizing one program with the Museum Educators of Southern California involved 1. developing a list of topics and speakers to approach, 2. finding willing museums to host an event for free, 3. arranging catering, 4. publicizing and promoting the event via e-mail, website, Facebook and printed flyers, 5. taking registrations and payments via PayPal, and, of course, 6. making a flurry of phone calls to assign tasks the day of the program and ensure that it ran smoothly. All board members were expected to attend as many programs as possible, to lend support and to network with members. Evaluations were distributed and scrutinized thoroughly after the program. It did take my free time, but it was enjoyable and meaningful.

Whom Are Boards Looking For?

A museum may have a varied collection of artifacts, some from ancient cultures and others of recent vintage, which can make for richly textured exhibitions. Committees are no different. It takes a wide range of people and skills to put on programs, publish a journal or organize a conference.

Some committees want leaders in the field with professional connections to help them book speakers for a symposium. Others need people who are skilled with logistics when organizing the registration for a workshop. All of them value people with Web and social media skills, as these are the most cost-effective ways to communicate with and grow membership. Not afraid of budgets or managing small amounts of money? Volunteer to serve as a treasurer on your local board. The most basic skills are the ones that are overlooked: answering e-mails and committing to attend meetings on the phone or in person and following through on tasks. Emerging professionals can make invaluable contributions to a committee by being present, being responsive and demonstrating a willingness to take initiative.

So I encourage you to take stock of what you have to offer and align it with the needs of the museum community. And as you discover the value in volunteering, you will see just how big your snowball can grow.

Afterword

Caitlin Kreiman Lill

Environmental Office Manager, Urbana Park District

I recently accepted my first full-time job in a museum. I had just finished my M.A. in museum studies, and had been working part-time in museums for several years when my current position became available. After my first few months at the museum, it was obvious that nothing so far had prepared me for a full-time management position, and while I was far from floundering, there was an obvious need for improvement. The essays in this section provide excellent examples of established museum educators who have been through this process before and the wisdom they've gained over time. In many cases, I wish I had had this information and guidance before I started so I might have avoided a few of the more common issues that challenge emerging educators.

McRainey's chapter reminds us that the educational theories we espouse for use with visitors are applicable to ourselves as learners as well—that we need to retain "a sense of wonder" and remember the power of "changing the context" of our work. She also comments that museum professionals need to be more open to ask "what if," a question that I find comes naturally to most emerging museum professionals. We are often passionate about "what if" ideas as we approach or begin our museum careers, but lose sight of them through the pressures of conformity and desires to be included in a new workplace, an issue that William Crow touches on (Chapter 7). In my personal practice, it's been easy so far to make sure that basic best practices are in place before moving forward with grand ideas and creativity; what I hope to remember over the next few years is to never lose sight of the need for innovation and flexibility in reaching our audiences.

When entering a new job as a museum educator, there are any number of things to learn about the position, not least of which is information about your new communities and audiences. Crow reminds us that there is another culture we must adjust to: that of the museum and our colleagues. Many of us emerging educators have a strong foundation in museum practices and are eager to influence our surroundings with our "what if" ideas. What we have to consider is whether we're truly "fluent" or if perhaps we've just taken a few "conversational" classes. Crow stresses that deep listening is key to communicating in the workplace, and that we need to be able to decode the language of our colleagues in order to seamlessly integrate ideas to achieve the mission of the museum. You may be tempted to pass over the "fill in the blanks" exercises at the end of the chapter as simplistic, but I can say from experience that these are exactly the sorts of scenarios that make up our interactions with new colleagues. Remember that knowing that there will be a new "language" to learn doesn't mean it won't take hard work and effort to become fluent. Also critical is to remember that every new volunteer, intern and staff member will encounter these same issues, and to approach them with patience and a willingness to be supportive.

Beverly Serrell's essay (Chapter 8) demonstrates another issue in communication and workplace environments: What happens when communication starts to break down? Our love for our institutions and missions can drive us beyond the usual passionate support for ideas we believe will be beneficial to our audiences and into the realm of encroaching on others' responsibilities and personalities. As Serrell says, it's already unlikely that all team members' thoughts will mesh harmoniously, and while disagreements are natural and can be dealt with calmly, we run the risk of alienating our colleagues if we don't learn to pick our battles. The success of a museum can be linked directly back to the internal cohesion and relationships, not just the power of the mission and vision.

Sheri Bernstein's essay (Chapter 9) speaks to me as a new staff member in a museum as I navigate my workplace and develop connections with my co-workers. The desire to be liked by my co-workers and to make connections with them has been high, but as a manager it's my responsibility to occasionally stand up for risky ideas that may not be popular with everyone. Bernstein's checklist of questions is one I'm sure I'll be referencing for years to come when faced with a difficult (potential) confrontation. Her advice for how to communicate diplomatically is also excellent, especially in downplaying your personal connection or credit for an idea.

Many emerging professionals love the work they do in their own museums, but are still left wondering how to give their careers an extra boost. I can say from experience that Sarah Marcotte's advice to volunteer for regional or national museum organizations is spot on. I always knew that my "job" wouldn't be the whole of my museum career, but hadn't been sure where to get started. My opportunity came during the formation of the Bay Area Emerging Museum Professionals group (BAEMP) through AAM. My version of saying "yes" couldn't have been easier: I agreed to collect e-mails from interested parties, and two hours later AAM had called to congratulate me on starting a regional EMP group, something I didn't really know I had just done. I embraced the opportunity, though, and haven't stopped saying "yes" yet. I've transitioned to being the editor-in-chief at the EMP blog, have a national network that includes dozens of emerging and established professionals, and am involved in setting the dialogue about the EMP movement.

Ultimately what these essays show is that your workplace culture and communication skills are critical to your success as a museum educator. Museum education departments must be willing to be open and sensitive to their colleagues, just as they would with any other of their audiences.

Things to Ponder:

1. Are there any "what if" ideas you've encountered in your career? What are some things emerging educators can do to help support or embrace "what if" ideas in their workplace?

2. Have you ever described a colleague as "speaking a different language?" If you have encountered tension that resulted from this, how did you resolve it? Could it have been resolved differently or better?

3. Consider your work style. Are you amiable and a pleaser? Or are you overly confrontational? How does this impact the way you communicate? How would you describe your direct supervisor or other co-workers?

Section 3: When Obstacles Arise

Chapter 11

You Made a Mistake. Now What?

Celeste DeWald

Executive Director
California Association of Museums

Very early in my career, when I was working at a small art and history museum, I coordinated a public program in collaboration with another nonprofit organization. It had taken me months to cultivate this relationship, and I was eager to see it lead to bigger and better projects. Unfortunately, in haste, I neglected to list the partnering organization in the press release before distributing it to the media. To make matters worse, I did not handle the situation well when they confronted me. I did not confess that it was my oversight because I was fearful that it would negatively impact our growing partnership—as well as reflect poorly on me. Despite my intent, this lack of transparency had the opposite result I had been hoping for: even though the program was well received, the partnering nonprofit organization chose not to pursue future collaborations. In hindsight, I believe my lack of responsibility and transparency contributed to this outcome. I did not create an environment of trust and accountability—which was the foundation we needed to take our partnership to the next level. This was one of those watershed moments for me in my career and it continues to guide me in my work today.

I know it sounds like a cliché, but the best teachers in my museum career have been the mistakes I have made. As you would suspect, I've learned how to avoid some of them and have practiced valuable problem-solving skills. My advice for emerging professionals, however, concerns a different aspect of making a mistake. What transpires in the moments after you discover your error? Do you ignore it, thinking no one will notice? Do you try to find a fall guy? Or do you "own it" and take responsibility? Personally, I have found that being proactive in taking responsibility for my actions (even when I would rather run the other way) has become a defining characteristic of my leadership style.

After I realize I have made a big mistake, my reaction is not unusual in those first few minutes. I usually have a sick feeling in my stomach, a fast heartbeat, a rise in body temperature and a face as red as a turnip. My mind races through possible solutions and, admittedly, some of them are not viable. I tell myself that everything is going to be okay, while I start to chew on my lower lip. I am not embarrassed to say that I have had several of these moments in the 20 years I have worked in the museum field. Although the scene may be different, some combination of this visceral response is present. Sometimes it is a relatively minor mistake, such as calling a donor by the wrong name. Other times, my mistake has had serious ramifications. I accept that we are all human and error comes with the territory. What I have learned along the way, however, is that what happens in these emotionally charged and vulnerable moments defines a person's leadership style and affects the work environment. When I have handled these situations well, the simple act of admitting that the mistake was mine and taking responsibility paved the way to finding a solution. I also believe it sent a message to my colleagues that I have integrity and want to be held accountable—both of which are characteristics I personally value in a leader.

My experience has also been that there is only one predictable result of scapegoating and ambiguity: a work environment that fosters distrust and a lack of accountability. I learned this lesson by having the misfortune of working for someone whose typical response to a problem was to deflect criticism rather than accept responsibility. I do not believe this individual had any malicious intent. Conversely this person probably thought that a strong leader should be a model of perfection and that strategic scapegoating would put the interests of the organization above those of individual employees. The result, however, was a work environment that bred fear and mistrust. People asked themselves, "If the head of the organization cannot be held responsible, why should anyone else?" Our leader was not modeling the behavior I felt was needed to encourage teamwork. Now when I hear anyone scapegoating another colleague, it makes me question that individual's perspective and honesty.

One of my "favorite" mistakes took place when I was the curator of education at the National Steinbeck Center. As the project director on a grant, I was responsible for the budget and was helping the director of development prepare a final report. Although I do not remember the specifics, I know I had made some sort of miscalculation in the expenditures. I was extremely nervous about admitting this mistake to my colleague and concerned about how the funder would respond. I had visions in my mind that the museum's reputation would suffer from my mistake and that we would never again receive another grant. Despite these fears, I knew it would be best to admit my mistake to the director of development and offer a couple of solutions. My colleague's response was more than I could have hoped for. She was generous and understanding and came up with a plan of action that involved meeting with the funder to find a mutually beneficial solution. With her support and others on our executive team, we were successful in turning a mistake into an opportunity to build our relationship with the funder, as well as to be transparent about our organization's decisions and needs.

It has not been my experience that people want to idolize leaders or hold them up to standards that are unrealistic or unattainable. Instead, they want to follow or support people who are real, with whom they can identify and can trust. Even though it may seem counterintuitive, revealing my own imperfections has oftentimes been my moment of strength as a leader.

Let's accept that all of us will make mistakes throughout our distinguished museum careers. Some mistakes will be big and others small—but it doesn't really matter. What matters is that you own that mistake and make it yours. These moments in your career will define you and reveal what kind of leader you are. With that as the guiding principle, these suggestions may help pave the way to finding a solution and growing from the experience:

1. Take responsibility when things go wrong. Be honest with yourself and others about what happened and what you could have done differently. Don't let someone else take the fall for your actions.

2. Take the initiative in offering solutions. If you played a part in creating the problem, this is your opportunity to be part of the solution.

3. Do not be shy in asking for assistance.

4. Consider what you could have done differently and how you will grow from the experience.

5. Be understanding when your colleagues make mistakes. Model the behavior you hope others will show you.

6. Don't dwell on any mistake, whether it is yours or someone else's. Shake it off and move forward.

Although one could argue that fostering an environment of trust and accountability starts at the top, I feel it is the responsibility of everyone on the team. If I want my colleagues, team members and volunteers to have ownership of their decisions and what they do, I need to model the behavior. It is important to me that I foster an environment where people are accountable and honest, and feel supported. I believe that how someone handles a mistake reveals a lot about that person. Anyone can make a mistake. But it is a strong sign of leadership to take responsibility and proactively seek a solution.

Chapter 12

Beware of Marriage Proposals

Sarah Alvarez

Director of Teacher Programs
Art Institute of Chicago

A bout three years into my career as a museum educator, I gave a Saturday afternoon highlights tour of the Art Institute. This was a regular occurrence for me and, after a few years of practice, I had begun to feel fairly confident in my abilities both as a public speaker and in managing a large group through the museum. I don't recall the specific route I took, but our final stop was Picasso's Cubist portrait, *Daniel-Henry Kahnweiler* (1910). After sharing some basic information about the style, subject and historical context of the painting, I thanked the group for their time and wished them a pleasant afternoon in the museum. Per usual, a few members of the group stayed on to ask me questions or share personal opinions about works of art on our tour.

One man had patiently waited for everyone else to ask their questions; when he was the last one to approach me, rather than quietly sharing his thoughts, he backed up a few steps, dropped to one knee, threw out his arms and rather loudly asked if I would marry him. On a Saturday afternoon, the museum and that particular gallery of early 20th-century European modern art were packed with visitors, many of whom had not been on the tour but were just perusing the paintings and sculpture on view. Needless to say, when this man shouted his proposal, it felt like every one of those visitors in the gallery turned to look. What was I, experienced with Picasso's Cubist period but not marriage proposals, supposed to do? While my flight instinct kicked in, I realized I couldn't just walk away. So I feigned a laugh and tried to get the man to stand up, while I jokingly remarked how funny he was and that I'd never before had such a heartfelt thanks for a highlights tour. I thanked him for his enthusiasm and, while walking backwards out of the gallery, explained that I needed to get back to my office. I never did see that particular visitor again, but his actions and my befuddlement at how to handle them have stuck with me.

While based in part on this specific and, only in retrospect, rather amusing experience, my personal motto of gallery teaching—"Beware of Marriage Proposals"—has evolved with time and a healthy dose of humility. Several early, sometimes awkward moments or surprising discoveries in my teaching career taught me that visitors may have distinctly different expectations of their museum experience—and of me as the facilitator of that experience—than I imagined. When I entered the field of museum education, fresh out of graduate school in art history, I had not considered that museum learning was as much, if not more, a social and very personal experience as an intellectual one.

To discern the motivations of your audience, or even just one member of your audience, you can simply just ask them. Or they may spring it on you at any given moment—although maybe not in such a dramatic way as the marriage proposal. However you discover them, I suspect you will find the range and nature of visitors' reasons enlightening. In the case of directly inquiring what someone is looking for in her museum experience, I recall a number of distinct responses. The first came from a woman whom I was specifically asking about her interest in a modern architecture exhibition she had just visited. She informed me that her primary reason for coming to the museum—and she did so frequently—was to see El Greco's *The Assumption of the Virgin* (1577–79) and to pray in front of it. Her visit to the architecture installation on that day was just a side note to her true motivation. This exchange took place literally just weeks after I began working at the museum and was indeed an early indicator to me of the diversity of visitors and reasons for viewing art that I would encounter in my new career. In my naïveté, I wondered both how such a secular place as an art museum could suffice as a church, of which there are so many in Chicago and nearby the museum, and how such a relationship with and reliance on that particular painting could develop. I never did get the answer to either question from that woman, but the story has remained in my memory.

Another instance occurred somewhat further along in my tenure after developing more of a rapport with a group of "regulars" who attend multiple gallery talks every week. I became curious about why (and how) they came to the museum so frequently and why they never seemed to mind hearing about the same works of art, over and over, even attending the same gallery talk repeatedly—and taking delight in correcting me when I misspoke! So of course, I just asked them. One group of men always seemed to show up and leave together, but otherwise their lives didn't intersect. For them, the gallery talk was a social event or medium they could rally around, and it gave them a sense of belonging that maybe they couldn't find elsewhere. Similarly an older woman who comes to the museum literally every day explains that her walk down Michigan Avenue to the Art Institute is her daily "constitutional." She lives alone, so the social nature of the gallery talk provides her something she needs emotionally.

There was a common thread among these responses: they all found a sense of connection and comfort in the repeated act of attending the tour and reaffirming what they already knew about works of art. Sure, they enjoyed learning new things and would often share their enthusiasm for new exhibitions or museum acquisitions. But underneath it all—or even overtly on the face of it—they found pleasure in their repeated museum experiences in the same way that some of us love to reread a favored book and revisit its cast of characters as if they were old friends. This was a clear indication of an emotional need and outcome from the services I was providing that I had truly not considered when I accepted the job—and, at that point, I'd never even read a book or article by John Falk!

My interactions over the years with these "regulars" bring to mind the other half of the "museum visitor expectation" equation (the first being what they expect to learn or experience): the visitor's hope or belief about me as the facilitator of that experience. What I think and expect to be a discrete interaction in the museum—a gallery talk—is truly much more in the eyes of certain visitors. Again, this was a surprise for me initially, and something with which I've had to come to terms. The "regulars" want to see me as their friend or pal. They want to connect with me and my colleagues, just as as they did with the works of art. They send us postcards from their travels and they hang out after each talk to chat and tell us about the latest exhibition they saw or lecture they attended. They act a bit like groupies. In addition to the "regulars" at the gallery programs, there is one in particular who rides the same commuter train as I do and has often wanted to sit with me for the 40-minute ride or walk with me the mile from the station to the museum (his office is near the museum). One might say this is just an occupational hazard of our work and, on occasion, I have had to be very blunt and explain that I am not available to talk, or walk and talk. On other occasions, I have also intentionally stepped out of view, moved to a different train car, or taken a slower or more circuitous walking route on the street. It is at these moments that I am reminded that, while I don't honestly expect a marriage proposal from this person, there are all sorts of expectations about the relationships we establish with visitors when we engage with them during a public program.

My anecdotes and comments might suggest that I am antisocial and uninterested in even the slightest form of informal chatter—or, alternately, that I have a totally magnetic personality that attracts all these visitors. Sorry to disappoint any readers, but neither of these things is true. Rather, I have had a series of experiences that has taught me what it really means to be an educator. If I think back to my own education, I admired my teachers for their knowledge and, in the best cases, I was inspired by their passion for their subject. These teachers motivated me to continue to learn and to love to learn. I've come to understand that as either classroom or museum educators, we not only transmit knowledge, but we can inspire, engage and even offer comfort and a sense of connection to our students.

Successful learning experiences are often just as social or emotional as they are intellectual. Humbly, I've also realized that my role in that experience is only one part. As with the woman who came to pray in front of El Greco's masterpiece, it was the art itself that motivated her—I had nothing to do with it. In the case of the others, who were actually participants in my tours, my role as educator became inextricably tied to the value that the art and the museum holds for them on a personal level. Over my career, I have come to appreciate the importance of these expectations and continually look for and experiment with teaching strategies that nurture such hopes. It motivates me to find room for improvement, even if it means that every so often I have to change train cars or walk backwards out of a gallery with a nervous smile on my face.

Chapter 13

Evolve as a Museum Leader: Be a Catalyst!

Paula Gangopadhyay

Chief Learning Officer
The Henry Ford

I started my museum career right out of graduate school at a small historical village in Michigan where I was the first and only professional staff member. I was "gung ho" as I saw the exciting possibility of turning all the theoretical knowledge I had acquired straight into practice. There were occasions when I would be in a business suit returning from a convention and visitor's bureau meeting on statewide tourism, and I would have to rapidly change into a 19th-century pioneer dress to give a tour of the only remaining toll-gate house in Michigan to 200 schoolkids. My first museum office was a cozy walk-in closet in a one-room schoolhouse. I nonchalantly drove around collecting boxes of "2D artifacts" from board members' homes with the vision of establishing a professional archive, per museum standards. I made my husband drive me to the distant countryside so I could buy old-fashioned wooden toys for the museum's summer camp program, and I burned the midnight oil to write 29 grants the very first year to fund innovative ideas.

Eighteen years later, I have the good fortune of being the chief learning officer at The Henry Ford, which attracts over 1.5 million visitors per year. We have a staff of more than 1,200, five fabulous sites that tell stories of American innovation, 26 million artifacts and a charter school with 500 high school students. I now have an office that is the envy of many. I held other great jobs in between as I went through my adventurous journey, even daring for a few years, as an informal education leader (with a museum background), to steer an intense school reform movement. There are great differences in the scope and scale of the jobs I have done, but the overall experience has many similar strands.

For young professionals like I was years ago, coming out of graduate school into the professional world full of experienced people, the biggest challenge is proving oneself and gaining the confidence of others in you as a leader. But I want first to define what "leadership" has meant to me right from the beginning. Leadership in my mind is not simply acquiring a bombastic title or a lot of authority within your institution, but gaining a distinctive, deep-rooted respect from your peers, subordinates, supervisors and the community *for what you contribute*. How do you carve a distinct role among so many talented and dedicated colleagues when sometimes it may seem there's no room for growth, resources or opportunities? Leadership opportunities normally take time to come by, and require an inordinate amount of patience and persistence. But there are subtle yet conscious steps that you can take to start positioning yourself as a leader—right from the onset of your career. I did it by being a catalyst.

Granted, the field of "education and public programs" within museums (which has been my forte) is often where people look for fresh ideas and visionary leadership. But I have applied the same approach when I worked in other administrative or consulting capacities. These catalytic experiences have not only provided me with practical scenarios where I have honed my own critical thinking, problem-solving and leadership skills, but allowed the organizations I worked for to take the leap of faith for exponential growth and sustainability. The most critical lesson in being a catalyst is that the leadership skills you acquire are transferable to a wide variety of situations and organizations. Being a catalyst is not an easy job, by any means.

You can evolve as a leader by being a catalyst, so don't be afraid to take the challenge.

I would like to share some lessons that I have learned throughout my career.

Push Boundaries

My personal urge to push boundaries manifested itself when I was getting my archival and museum studies certification degree from Duquesne University in Pittsburgh. As part of our degree completion, we were to seek out professional internships with area cultural organizations. Till then I had not decided the path within the museum profession I wanted to pursue. Like a classic grad, I was confused, so this was going to be an exploration. My first choice for the museum internship was the Carnegie Museum, as I knew that the endorsement would take me far in my future career. But I was told that no intern from our university's program had been accepted in the past, so it would be an impossible feat. I wanted to be the change agent for my university and challenge the situation that existed—or at least try. I called and asked for an appointment with the collections manager. Maybe I was plain lucky, but they called me in, alerting me that they could not promise anything. The interview went really well. I was relaxed and non-pushy, and conveyed with confidence that they would gain as much as I would by offering me this rich learning experience, essential for any emerging museum professional. I shared my sincerity about learning and humbly sought their mentorship. I was accepted. My professor was extremely proud of me, as I helped open the door for his future interns into this world-renowned institution. Incidentally the experience played a huge role in my future career choice. The internship made me conclude that with my personality I did not want to pursue a collections-related job, as I wanted something where I could work more with people versus solitary researching and organizing.

Throughout my career, I have pushed boundaries—for myself, my staff and peers. I try to facilitate among people I work with, to re-imagine, look out-of-the-box, think holistically, challenge the norm and be creative. The concepts, products and partnerships that have evolved as a result of the "pushing the boundary" approach have inspired the admiration of many, and have helped me stand out as a visionary leader.

Take Time and Go Slow

The challenge that comes with pushing boundaries and coming up with new ideas is that you are bound to ruffle feathers, miff egos, stir emotions, step into other's territory and automatically create resistance. But be true to yourself. Accept the fact that for catalysts, resistance is normal. The solution to successfully turning the resistance into acceptance and eventually admiration is by going *slow and steady*. Don't attempt to turn the world upside down as soon as you get somewhere. Be sensitive and dialogue with people (even with those who may seem like your biggest critics). Try not to be judgmental even if you hear all sorts of stories about certain people. Form your own opinions, but only after studying people deeply for a while. I have always used a self-created, four-pronged approach to make things happen from the onset:

1. Keep what's going well.

2. Infuse some critical enhancements to make the "better" the "best."

3. Create and launch some paradigm-shifting ideas, a.k.a. "differentiators."

4. Be brave about eliminating redundant or non-productive programs, but only after objective assessment and candid dialogue focusing on institutional needs.

Do all of this in a slow and steady manner. Most people are unsuccessful, and their well-intentioned efforts fizzle out because they start with number four, which is deleting, first.

Scale Your Projects and Learn from Failures

Most of the time, implementation of an idea fails because we scope it out too big. Start small with solid planning, implementing, collecting data and molding it into better form. In my career I have relied heavily on the concept of prototyping, tightly backed by an aggressive expansion plan.

Don't be afraid to jump-start ideas, and most importantly don't get bogged down by those who like to plan for years, as their ideas may never take off or become obsolete by the time they do get off the ground. Catalysts are risk-takers, and an essential part of the process is learning from failures. Anticipate that your critics will slam you, so be proactive and positively alert them upfront that realistically, failure may happen, but it should not put an end to the game-changing process you are trying to lead.

Build Your Energy Brigade

To sustain as a catalyst, the essential life breath is positive energy. Identify a few supporters, not just inside the institution but in the larger community, who will give you that shot in the arm when negative energies may be draining your motivation. Your leadership role is to veer through challenges by being resourceful, nimble and positive. Over the years, I have built my own "Energy Brigade" of teachers, colleagues, people I have met in conferences and panels, community partners and even consultants I have hired or worked with. They have been there for me when I have needed them for a boost to keep going. Appreciate these people by involving them and being in communication with them, as your energy in turn empowers them. This group is your biggest, though unofficial support system.

Be a Thought Leader

The most critical role of a catalyst is to shape change. At times you may feel frustrated that you have a lot of responsibility but no authority. But don't let the tactical bother you. Consciously climb to a strategic plateau where fame, glory, recognition, media coverage should not matter. What should matter is people's respect and, most importantly, their including you in the strategic institutional decision-making process. The sense of gratification you get from that sort of inclusive leadership is far more satisfying than any salary raise, big title or lots of authority. This feeling is subtle yet powerful, and nurturing for your mental and physical health and well-being. It makes you love what you do.

Lastly always remember that as educators we are the foundation of any museum or cultural institution. We have an undeniably important responsibility towards the overall community. You are a leader, as you can and will make a difference. Your learning should never end as you go through your career, but you have the important role of helping others constantly learn, too.

Chapter 14

Sometimes You Have to Be
a Little Subversive

Ted Lind

Former Deputy Director for Education
Newark Museum

S ubversion is defined as an attempt to transform an established social order, its structures of power, authority and
hierarchy. Does this sound too radical for museum educators? Are we content with the status quo? How can you best
activate change when there appears to be strong resistance to
it? I have used slightly gentle subversion at times in order to get
something meaningful accomplished. My belief in the use of
subversion was confirmed in an effort to strengthen museum
learning for family visitors.

Earlier in my career as a museum educator, I was working at an art
museum that had made a commitment to expanding and strengthening
its service to youth and families, especially through the development of
compelling leisure-time activities (weekends) at the museum. In fact, I had
worked closely with the museum's director and the development officers to
devise a plan for a multi-year, family-learning study that received funding
support from the Institute of Museum and Library Services. As the curator of education at the museum, I had also involved stakeholders in the

community and a team of consultants who were all going to assist in the process of engaging family audiences. It became quite clear early on in the study that the most important element of the family visit to the museum was when they would go through the galleries on their own. Yes, the museum had highly effective programs for visiting families, such as guided tours, storytelling, performances, "make and takes," festivals and more, but the independent visit left families feeling a little lost. Unless they were guided by a live person or used a printed gallery guide or "scavenger hunt," the families felt they did not belong in the galleries.

It became clear that the museum needed to provide opportunities for family visitors to become more excited about being in the galleries, more comfortable and more engaged in enjoyable learning. Families in the study had also demonstrated how much they appreciated hands-on experiences and how rewarding and memorable these experiences were for their "quality time" together. During the course of the study, the museum was also developing a prototype for a family learning center, to be located in a recently vacated space that was the former café. It was an excellent location near the museum's auditorium and had access to a wet area, food service and a small adjacent community gallery. The only drawback was that it was far away from the main galleries and could be seen by some as another "education ghetto."

The prototype hummed along nicely. The center included rotating exhibits, an art-making area, a small library and an area where brochures and other printed matter could be picked up. Families loved the space, and it was used constantly. Many became repeat visitors, always looking for something new and exciting to do.

Based on the first year of the study, it seemed appropriate to begin developing some opportunities for families to have interactive experiences in the museum's main galleries, too—and not simply isolate this type of learning to the exhibits and workshop areas of the emerging family center. How could we do this? What models were out there for us to look at? With considerable thought and review of best practice models elsewhere (e.g., Denver Art Museum), we decided to focus our energies on an upcoming special exhibition being organized by the Hood Museum at Dartmouth

College. The exhibition featured art and artifacts from ancient Greece and interpreted them as resources to study the societal role of children in this distant culture. The exhibition included many references to Greek myths and legendary characters. Many fine examples of ceramics, metalwork and sculpture were highlighted. The thesis of the exhibition seemed the perfect vehicle for connecting with families, as well as organizations that oversee the interests of families and young children. The first version of the exhibition at the Hood Museum was strengthened by an interactive learning area that recreated an ancient Greek home, filled with touchable replicas. A visit by our team to the exhibition convinced us that we should do something similar for our visitors.

At my museum we developed a plan for an interactive space that would be right at the entrance to the exhibition (smaller than the Hood Museum's, due to space restrictions, but still substantial). Initially the curator and designer responsible for installing the exhibition supported the plan. However, I don't think they realized the full extent of what we were planning—we desired to respond to the needs we had discovered in our family learning study. We really wanted to test the value of creating a "discovery area" within an exhibition. Two months before the exhibition was scheduled to open (with our interactive learning area), the curator called me to his office and told me that there would not be enough room for the discovery area. My education colleagues and I were devastated. His decision was not brought to the exhibition team or to the director. The educators had been promoting this new approach to our community—groups interested in early childhood education, family issues and child development. What were we supposed to tell them? They were expecting the exhibition to be "family friendly."

To shut down this emerging new space without any discussion was not good, but it wouldn't be appropriate to approach the director with this "error in judgment"—the culture at this museum would not allow it. Instead we decided to be a little subversive. Along with some of my colleagues who work with family visitors, I wanted to demonstrate that we were trying to find another space in the museum that might accommodate the space—a willing compromise, if you will. We set out one morning with rulers and measuring tapes to locate a potential space not too far from the exhibition galleries, but in a major public area. We knew the director would see us engaged in this staged work, and we realized we would arouse his curiosity. Of course, he soon discovered what we were doing. After seeing us sprawled on the floor, we were surprised and delighted when he indicated that the discovery area *must* be in the exhibition proper and not isolated in a remote space. The curator and the designer were a little put off, but we indicated that most of the details for the learning area would be handled by the education staff, and they agreed to let us move forward. Our mild subversion had worked.

Once the exhibition opened, complete with the discovery area, our next step was to assess the value of the space for visitors during the three-month run of the exhibition. We also created complementary, hands-on experiences in the family learning center and a printed family guide. We hoped that the evaluation of the space would confirm its positive family impact. We were pleased when family visitors told us they loved the space and the ways it helped them connect to the ancient artworks on display. The museum's security guards even noted how valuable the space was for visitors with children; they were impressed with how they saw families interacting. The whole venture turned out to be very successful, leading to plans for future projects.

As each temporary special exhibition was developed from this point on, there was discussion about how interactive learning areas would enhance the visitor experience for families but also for all visitors. The curators began to think of interactive learning in their exhibitions as an essential ingredient. And visitors began to expect to see these opportunities in the exhibitions. Eventually I had the chance to work with the museum's development department and some very generous individuals to create an endowment for interactive learning that would enable the museum to design interactive learning "stations" in the permanent collection galleries.

The culture of each museum is different. But in art museums, the ultimate decisions about what takes place in the galleries are often made by the curators. Even though a team effort (curators, educators, designers, marketers, fundraisers, etc.) in exhibition development is embraced by a museum, it can be difficult, if not impossible, to convince others of the value of intellectual access for visitors of all ages and backgrounds. In this case, our meager subversion worked better than attempting to take the curator and designer head-on. This approach may not work in all situations, but it is an option that should be considered when and if you need it.

Use subversion sometimes. It can upset the culture and the power structure, but may, in the long run, help you serve your audiences more effectively.

Afterword

K. Tierney Sneeringer

Luce Foundation Center Program Specialist
Smithsonian American Art Museum

I wonder if internships and graduate programs should consider implementing some sort of hidden camera situation like the TV shows Candid Camera and Punk'd. While this is admittedly an unorthodox approach to learning the ropes in a museum, nobody knows how they will respond in high-stress situations, and this would provide learners a safe opportunity to navigate obstacles. I would most likely hate this exercise, but think it would be incredibly helpful since I am still unsure of how I respond in these situations, even after being in the museum field for nearly five years.

I wonder how I handle mistakes and obstacles. I have certainly had those sweat-induced, I-am-going-to-panic reactions similar to the one that Celeste DeWald describes in the first chapter in this section. I have also learned how to better navigate uncomfortable situations with visitors and have learned more about the museum's culture and power structure. I am unable to recount, however, how I have responded to obstacles. Was I calm and collected? Or was my discomfort obvious to those around me? This section has certainly made me reflect on these moments in my career.

While all four authors describe a different type of career obstacle and how they handled it, all of the chapters in this section highlight the importance of confidence and transparency when overcoming obstacles. I was also reminded often of the lessons from the first section, "Climbing the Ladder": learn from each experience and be adaptable with your skills. Paula Gangopadhyay echoed the sentiments in Tinworth's chapter when she said, "The most critical lesson in being a catalyst is that the leadership skills you acquire are transferable in a wide variety of situations and organizations." Basically, we need to be chameleons, ready to change colors for each unique situation/environment.

Transferable skills are invaluable, but so is understanding your environment as both a museum educator (with visitors) and professional (with your colleagues). Alvarez discusses how she was empowered as an educator once she understood how visitors interacted with the museum. Possessing the smallest insight into visitors' lives enabled her to better understand the different types of connections people form in museums. It made me wonder about my own experiences with repeat visitors and how to engage them. Did the mother/son couple who had already attended one of my tours find my unprepared talk (at their request) on my favorite artworks enjoyable, or were they there mainly to be with each other? Knowing how visitors use your space will help you become a better educator and navigate those tricky moments when you are put on the spot.

Institutional knowledge is also needed when obstacles arise. Ted Lind provides us with the perfect example of how an insider's knowledge enabled him and his team to successfully complete their work. If they had not been "subversive," they would never have been able to be a catalyst in their institution and change the status quo. This is hard as an emerging professional. It takes time to understand the nuances of your institution's culture and power structure. You only start to obtain this knowledge once you are confident of your contribution to your institution.

Confidence is a must in order to push boundaries, be a catalyst and successfully navigate obstacles. DeWald, Alvarez, Gangopadhyay and Lind were all able to overcome mistakes and difficult situations because they were confident in their abilities, either as a leader or as museum educator. Each author does an excellent job pinpointing the qualities one needs to possess and elicit from others when obstacles occur: honesty, humility, respect, admiration, creativity and ingenuity. I also appreciated Gangopadhyay's addition of the "Energy Brigade." It is sometimes too easy to feel defeated and negative, especially in the face of difficult times. I think I am going to take her advice and build my own "Energy Brigade." Who's in?

Things to Ponder:

Have you made a mistake at work? How did you respond? Are you proud of how you handled the situation?

1. How can you foster an environment of trust and accountability among your colleagues?

2. How can you personally learn more about your institution's visitors?

3. Whom would you recruit to be in your "Energy Brigade"?

4. When you have been told "no" to a project you truly believe in, how could you have employed subversive tactics to get the job done?

Section 4: Looking Forward

Chapter 15

Yes, You Should Go to Grad School

Ben Garcia

Head of Interpretation
Phoebe A. Hearst Museum of Anthropology

Yes, you're right: experience and good instincts are often better qualifications for a job than a graduate degree. And yes, you're right: academics too often ignore the messy realities of real museum work. And sure, you are correct: sometimes that colleague or supervisor or director who holds an M.A. or M.S. or Ph.D. really *is* missing the point, is full of it, is completely clueless. But despite all that, and no matter how great you are at your job, if you are asking yourself (or your friends) time and again whether you should go to grad school, the answer is "yes."

This, coming from a person who does not like going to school, someone who flunked out of college at age 20 and who finally graduated with a bachelor's at 30. It wasn't that I was stupid—and I'll spare you the embarrassment of a grown man proffering his high school GPA and SAT scores as evidence—but I was disconnected from that clarity that Marjorie Schwarzer (Chapter 5) rightly suggests is so important to meaningful success. By the time I had entered the field of museum education in my early 30s, the last thing I wanted to do was continue my own formal education.

But there I was in an entry-level position, where, after a few years, I began complaining about the fact that an advanced degree was necessary to move forward in the profession. After all, I believed that I was as smart as my colleagues with master's degrees, and I scoffed at the idea that an advanced degree would somehow make me better at my job. I remember with some embarrassment saying to a tactful and very patient colleague (who held an M.A. in museum studies) that there was nothing you could learn in grad school that you couldn't learn on the job. Attending my first National Art Education Association museum conference (and getting a glimpse of a world to which I wanted to belong) persuaded me to take the plunge and apply for a master's program in museum education and leadership.

I am here to tell you that not only did going to graduate school make me better at my job, it changed my career trajectory, aligned me with my passion and gave me a vision for what I want to do in this field that holds strong five years after graduating. Ignoring for a moment the fact that degree inflation is a reality in the museum field (I recently conducted an informal survey of the American Alliance of Museums' job site and found that about 70 percent of the jobs in museum education required a master's degree or higher), and that Census Bureau statistics show that people with advanced degrees will earn considerably more per year than those holding a bachelor's degree, attending the right graduate program at the right time can be the academic equivalent of unplugging from the Matrix. You will see the larger context for your work, find the thinkers whose ideas connect to and advance your own and give you the language and theoretical framework to describe something that you may have known only instinctually before.

The Right Time

If you are regularly asking yourself or others in your life whether you should go back to school, it is likely that some part of your mind has decided that, in fact, you should. I have three clarifying questions to help the other parts catch up. If you answer all three with a "yes," then this is likely the time to find that right program and get going.

1. Are you, or have you been, employed in the field?

Some readers of this book are probably not yet employed. With job prospects for recent graduates about as encouraging as those for the Sorbonne's graduating class of 1788, many folks enter graduate programs as a way of waiting for the job market to heat up (or for the revolution to come). In some cases, this is the right choice—especially when the person is clear about her or his desired career trajectory. But for those readers who, like me, will take a little longer to find their passion, taking on the additional debt burden of a graduate museum program without spending a few years actually engaged in the work of museums is not advisable. Instead, if you cannot find employment at a museum, I would advise taking a page from Sarah Marcotte (Chapter 10) and spend some time volunteering for one. If you are not newly out of an undergraduate program but have been working in another field and are considering a change, I'd suggest the same: secure a job or spend some time volunteering at a museum before applying for a graduate program. The learning that occurs in the classroom at a good graduate program can be amazing. However, it is not a substitute for the experience of working as part of a museum that is trying to find (or has found), a sustainable model for success. Bringing together the research-based knowledge of the classroom and the experience-based knowledge of a workplace (good, bad, large or small) is plain alchemy: there is simply no more powerful educative experience than the application of theory to practice.

2. Do you spend some part of each work week talking to colleagues or loved ones (or increasingly nervous-looking strangers) about how insanely off-base and out of touch your supervisor/department head/director is?

Speaking with others about the shortcomings and failings of the leadership in your department or organization can be—let's face it—fun. Complaining about the workplace can be an important part of developing workplace relationships; it can help a person figure out how to address a problem (or work around one) and, in my experience, insightfully criticizing the boss (and it always feels insightful) can provide an energizing boost of righteousness. But griping about the leadership is the last bastion of those who feel powerless, and while it has some useful functions, it can turn ugly pretty quickly. The satisfying boost will, if a regular occurrence, become increasingly discouraging. You have probably had the experience of avoiding that bitter colleague at work—the one who would rather complain and be unhappy than find a better situation. Before you become that person (you know just how close you are to that point, and, trust me, so do your co-workers), take an action on your own behalf, one that is truly empowering. If you are complaining about your job more than occasionally, you are likely either in the wrong job, bored and ready to learn something new, or in need of some additional skills. The right graduate program will address all of these possibilities. Graduate school can be the perfect place to gain the skills that you need to assess what the right next professional step should be and to succeed in that next step.

3. Can you afford to go back to school?

This question can only be addressed individually. The nature of the program, the choice of institution and your resources will be the factors that answer this question for you. However, if your response to this is a knee-jerk "no," I think it is worth exploring. There are creative solutions to the problem of cost. Programs exist that accommodate the needs of full- or part-time working individuals so that you can continue to earn an income while in school. There is at least one reputable distance-learning program in museum studies (through the University of Leicester in the UK), and costs for distance learning are considerably less than for attending a program in person. And there is a wide range of costs associated with attending even full-time graduate programs. I chose a program designed for working museum professionals and I commuted to my monthly, weekend-long classes out of state for two years. There was a cost associated with the travel, but because I was able to continue to earn a wage while attending, and because the program was (relatively) modestly priced, I ended up with a total of $36,000 in student loans at the end of it. For a museum professional with no outside means of financial support, I would not recommend taking on much more than $50,000 of additional debt.

Because museum jobs are not going to provide the kind of financial dividends that jobs in law or business might, keeping your debt load balanced with realistic earning potential is essential to your future well-being. That said, you will be able to earn a higher wage with an advanced degree both because of the new skills it provides (which make you eligible for better jobs) and because employers generally expect to pay more to a candidate with a master's or Ph.D. than to one without for the same job. Though results vary, in my case the skills I gained in graduate school had a direct correlation to the jobs I secured after I finished the program (and the additional income has more than offset my monthly student loan payment). Granted, a student loan is not something to take on lightly. It will be with most of us for decades. Finding the right program will make all the difference between a financial burden that feels like an investment and one that feels like a millstone around your neck.

The Right Program

The right program is the program you can afford; the one in the right discipline; and, most important, one that is aligned with your values. Believe it or not, the question of what subject area to focus on is less important than that of alignment with your values. An affordable program in line with your values will give you the advantage in almost any future job. If you are on the fence about whether to do a program in education, in a content area like history or in management, you probably need to wait a little longer until your vision for your career becomes clearer. If you are certain that this is the right time and still are on the fence about the "what," go for a more general program like museum studies or nonprofit management. In these programs you will gain the big ideas that you can later apply to a number of jobs and environments.

The way to find the right graduate school, of course, will have a lot to do with your desired field(s) of study and your resources. This chapter will not be able to direct you to the specific place; however there is a reliable method for selecting the right program (beyond logistics) that can be applied by anyone considering this next step: *look at the programs at which the people whose ideas you admire teach (or taught) or at those they attend (or attended).*

If you are favorably impressed by colleagues, mentors, conference panelists or authors, find out where they did their studies. Ask to speak with them about their alma mater and you will quickly find out if they attribute any of their awesomeness to that experience. Maybe you can't always trust your instincts when it comes to the people to whom you are attracted (a topic for a wholly different article), but you *can* trust your instincts when it comes to the people whose ideas attract you. Research those programs and find out where their current graduates are working. Look at the philosophical underpinnings of the program and decide if they are a fit with yours. Chances are that if someone you admire is associated with the place, it will be a good fit for you.

In my case I heard a panelist at that National Art Education Association museum conference speak about the responsibility of museums to invest in staff development and to encourage staff to grow and to move on (and out, if need be). She said that we were in this for a bigger goal than our individual museums' success. Her view was that museum education departments shared a responsibility to raise the level of professionalism in the field as a whole. This was a new concept for me at the time and one that I found deeply compelling. When I found out that the panelist was an instructor and advisor at Bank Street College, I decided to apply there. Six months later I was in New York City sleeping on my cousin's cat-hair-covered sofa and attending my first class. And, boy, was it the right fit!

The right graduate program will change your life professionally (and, for some, personally). It does what all good education aspires to do: it takes a person who sees the world one way and opens that person to new and bigger possibilities. As an educator at an art museum, I found entering a program for professionals from a broad spectrum of museums to be a revelation, and it expanded my view of what types of museums I could work in. I learned from Lou Casagrande, a guest lecturer and, at the time, CEO of the Boston Children's Museum, that a leader "walks the periphery of an organization," keeping one eye focused inward and one outward. This changed my perspective from one focused just on my department and my museum to one that encompassed the field. I began to get involved in national organizations and worked with colleagues across the country and internationally. I saw similar shifts in the perspectives of my classmates who went on to take leadership roles and to broaden their possibilities.

Beyond the big paradigmatic shifts that occur for students in grad programs, there is a very practical outcome to be gained from the right program: the ideas that people generate—through readings, exercises and assignments—can inform their work for years to come in a tangible way. My master's thesis became the basis of several panel presentations at national conferences, as well as the source of two published articles. As my responsibilities have broadened in the positions I have held since attending grad school, the courses in management and leadership, development and marketing have taken root—two, three, five years after graduation. My former classmates and program advisors now form a wide network of colleagues I can call upon for assistance, moral support, references and just great conversation. The right graduate program will equip you to achieve professional clarity and success and, as my colleague Sheri Bernstein phrased it (Chapter 9), to "kick [some serious] ass!"

Chapter 16

You Don't Have to Be Married to Your Work

Elee Wood, Ph.D.

Associate Professor of Museum Studies and Education, Indiana University
Public Scholar of Museums, Families, and Learning,
The Children's Museum of Indianapolis

When I left my first museum position, my coworkers created a mini-exhibit about what I had contributed to the institution over the years. Included was a time sheet that recorded "26 gajillion" hours. It struck a chord with me. Do I work too much? Am I married to my work? My colleagues recognized (and still do) that I work more than I should, most of the time. It's not so much that I'm married to my work, but that I have high expectations for what I do and how that work reflects who I am as a professional. I love what I do. Importantly, though, I still get eight hours of sleep a night, go on vacations, contribute to the profession, and make a difference for my co-workers and the places I work. Finding the right balance between who you are, what you do and what you want to be known for can be a tricky prospect when you are at the beginning of your career. If you start out with some good, healthy expectations about how to balance your work with other experiences that help keep you sane and satisfied, you will be on the road to success.

Obviously, with 26 gajillion hours logged in a single week, I was starting off my career thinking I could accomplish everything in the time allotted. It took a while for me to realize that no matter how much time I spent on projects, there would always be more work that could be done. No matter how many projects I completed to my satisfaction, another one was coming up. One of the biggest challenges in getting yourself established in the museum field is having experience, and the way you get experience is through working on lots of projects and taking on new opportunities—and doing your best work on all of them. On the flip side, taking on projects and opportunities means more work to be done. So given all of this, how in the world are you supposed to do all your work in 40 hours a week? The simple answer is: you can't. There will always be too much work to be done, and never enough time to get it all done well.

There is a difference between being married to your work and loving your work. I am lucky that I have a job that I love, but that has not always been the case. Lots of times work is hard and feels impossible. I look for aspects of a job that I really like, and this is what drives me to continue to be involved and go beyond what might be expected of me on projects. Having a sense of balance between what I have to do and what I want to do is part of how it works. The big idea here is about commitments: in a marriage, you make some commitments to another person—about yourself and your partner, usually in some kind of vow about loyalty and love. In your work commitments, you still have to think about yourself and your partner (that is, your employer), but those commitments aren't necessarily the same as loyalty and love. Instead your commitments to this partner are about excellence and quality (well, and maybe some loyalty). Your commitments to yourself are ones of sanity and happiness (and, ideally, some love, too). I've come to depend on three strategies to help me make the right level of commitment: knowing how you work, knowing what drives your work, and keeping clear boundaries and setting priorities.

Knowing How You Work

In my first job as a salaried museum staff member, we had to submit weekly time sheets recording our hours worked. My supervisor laughed when I submitted a timesheet with 57 hours in a 40-hour workweek. "You know you don't get paid for that extra time, don't you? Just put down 40 and don't worry about it," she said. That made me pause. I didn't think that it was a good idea to just let it look like I worked 40 hours, because someone needed to see how much time it actually took to do the work! I decided not to change the hours, because I realized that I should pay better attention to how much time I was spending on my work.

A really good strategy for thinking about how you work is to keep a time log. If you have a daily calendar, keep track of how much time you spend reading your e-mail, chatting with co-workers, taking phone calls, going to meetings, preparing for meetings, running programs, etc. I discovered some things about myself that were useful in time management that I still use to this day. I realized that I had no idea how much time it really took me to write a report or to get ready to deliver a program. Keeping a log helped me see that I spent more time in "getting ready" than I did in producing the work. I had to think about what this meant for me and how I could change it. I don't think this helped me shave off any of those extra 17 hours I worked in a week, but it helped me think about how to focus my time and know where I had a tendency to lose time. (Those daily visits to the candy shop around the corner did help my emotional state, but they took a half hour out of my day!)

Knowing What Drives Your Work

I've done some crazy things in my museum career—riding in an elevator with a llama, scooping out pickles to help kids create their own pickle-a-saurus, spending the night in the museum with hundreds of Girl Scouts. All of these things were fun, but at the same time they required a commitment of time from me. What mattered to me in those moments was that I was able to create a memorable experience at the museum. Similarly there were times when working on a new exhibit project or an audience study required a lot of extra work, but it was work that I liked to do and it energized me.

Other responsibilities, like working on budgets, were a struggle—especially when I had to find a way to reduce the budget by 10 or 15 percent! These tasks were challenging, but not as much fun. They drew on a skill base that I had not fully developed. It was times like these when I felt compelled to take work home with me so that I could get it done. I'd find myself at home late into the night, still trying to wrestle numbers into spreadsheets—and not getting any closer to a resolution than when I left the office! I felt compelled to do this work so that I would look like a dedicated professional. The problem was, I didn't really do any better by taking the work home with me. I quickly realized that taking work home that you don't like isn't fun. It was hard to tell myself that I didn't have to do the work at home, but it was also important for me to realize that time away from work is what recharges me and helps me stay sane and happy. So I decided that if I took work home, it would only be because it would be enjoyable for me. It had to be projects that would get me excited and interested, and propelled my interests and ideas further.

Boundaries and Priorities

Having boundaries and priorities for your work and personal time is crucial to keeping yourself from falling into the trap of feeling like you can't get away. Remember when I said I got eight hours of sleep every night? Well, that's a priority for me! I came to realize that I do much better work when I am well rested, and I happen to be one of those people who needs eight (and, ideally, nine) hours of sleep to be productive. When I'm productive I can get a lot of work done and I don't get sick as often. I have also made it a priority to have dinner with my spouse every night. With a family (even if it's your pet), these priorities are easier to enforce because family members get pretty good at reminding you. Those priorities are about my leisure time, and in my work it is similar. I think about what must be done and then figure out (since I know how I work and what drives me) when and how I can accomplish a task. Even though I procrastinate as much as the next person, I still like to stay ahead of deadlines. By making it a priority to get projects done just one day ahead of the deadline, I feel like I can better maintain my boundaries.

Boundaries are best when you consistently reiterate them to yourself and to others, as necessary. For example, I make a point of not responding to work e-mails after a certain time. Some people don't answer their phones or even look at e-mail after work hours. It is really important to find time to "unplug" yourself from the constant stream of requests. Unless it's truly an emergency, the project will still be there for you to work on tomorrow. Remember, there's never enough time to do it all, so you don't need to break your neck to get there!

Saying "I Do"

I'll close by repeating that there's no end of work that can be done. To get ahead you have to be noticed, you have to do good work and earn your stripes. But you don't have to do this by working all the time. Learn how to manage your time, understand what excites you about your work and what doesn't. Decide what your boundaries are and stick to them. When you begin to get settled in to your job, you'll start to see the ebbs and flows of the work. You'll get into a rhythm that helps you know where to commit, how to prioritize and ultimately how you can manage to have a life outside of work. For as many hours as you work in a day or a week, or even a career, the commitment you make is first and foremost to yourself. Ask yourself what matters. Think about what you can do to keep yourself sane and happy, committed and loyal. Before long you'll come to realize that being married to your work is not necessary. If you keep to your boundaries, when someone asks you if you love your job, you can still answer, "I do."

Chapter 17

Life Is Short, So Seize the Moment and Go with Your Instincts

Marie Bourke, Ph.D.

Keeper, Head of Education
National Gallery of Ireland

You that would judge me, do not judge alone
This book or that, come to this hallowed place
Where my friends' portraits hang and look thereon;
Ireland's history in their lineaments trace;
Think where man's glory most begins and ends,
And say my glory was I had such friends.
　　　—W. B. Yeats, "The Municipal Gallery Revisited,"
　　　　New Poems (Dublin: Cuala Press, 1938), stanza 7.

When an invitation came to provide some helpful hints for colleagues in museums—what James Joyce might call "the reality of experience"—I felt that the reflections should be simple, practical and forged "in the smithy of my soul" so they would be genuine.[1]

That extra something called "judgment and instinct."

The occasions when museum professionals make decisions that are called instinctive or good judgment are those normally born of experience. These practitioners are committed to their jobs (having vested years in degrees and training), are passionate about public engagement and the collections, and are optimistic about the institution's future. They have expectations of working on projects that will stretch their abilities and test their decision-making powers. This picture is rounded off by the everyday inter-action with colleagues that is such an important feature of museum life. To paraphrase Yeats, our blessing is we have such friends.

Although everyone knows that the museum is led from the top down, there are moments when everyone on the team has to make a decision—fast. As life is not perfect, and we are the most imperfect element of it, the potential for mistakes or even failure is high. But failure can be a powerful learning tool. In addition, the benefits of being surrounded by bright, con-fident, ambitious people with whom problems can be shared ensures that while the environment is both competitive and collegial, it provides a useful learning resource and is never dull. Why, then, do people say a museum is a wonderful place to work? Because, though experience is continuous, once the basic training and experience are obtained, museum practitioners learn to trust their judgment and enjoy the pleasure of successful "instinctive" decision-making.

The notion that life is short has to do with the many inconsequential things that happen in the museum and absorb a lot of time. At its core is the fundamental understanding that the museum is *for people* and houses collections *for the public*. The really important stuff, therefore, has to do with the quality of the visitor's experience and interaction with the collec-tions. It's easy to forget that. The contemporary poet Paul Durcan's reaction to Francis Bacon's pictures at the Tate—they "lit up the gloom of life and turned my eyesight inside out"—provides a sharp reminder not to neglect that sense of wonder and surprise.[2] We must shake ourselves out of con-cerns over management meetings, catalogue entries, hanging plans and staff cutbacks, because dwelling on these things just makes life shorter. The work ethic I find useful is to use good judgment and sound instinct, and when that points in a direction, seize the moment and act on it.

Where Do Good Judgment and Instinct Come From?

The ability to trust one's judgment and be guided by one's instinct comes from experience. This involves the time and energy put into studying and assessing situations and working hard to improve them. Included are the quiet conversations in corridors, when you have the chance to encourage and support your colleagues, or listen to their stories and thank them for their work. It comes from the research and preparation that goes into solving a problem and seeing it through to resolution, ensuring everything functions on time and on budget. It also encompasses the late hours and weekends that go into producing strategies and publications that you present as simple and effortless. It even includes rare moments between meetings when you are the beneficiary of wonderfully perceptive insights. This experience that comes from hard work, talent and just a bit of luck helps museum practitioners to develop the confidence that leads to good judgment and instinct.

How Does It Work?

Consider the *Exploring Art Project*, comprising a handbook on art, a touring exhibition on "art and the environment," and a teacher-training program with student worksheets. All the key questions had been answered. Was the project solid? Were there expertise and sponsorship to deliver? Was the team capable of seeing it through to fruition? How would the project benefit the the museum as well as the public? Good judgment and a sound instinct that this was a worthwhile enterprise got it off to a start, underpinned by research demonstrating the need for professional teaching materials that explained how museums worked and how the collections could be used in the school. Skip forward to the project launch, when it emerged that while the handbook was positively received, the worksheet program—created as a tool for teachers to use in the classroom—was not. An evaluation revealed that had closer attention been paid to the students' comments, the result would have been imaginative worksheets. This example shows that the judgment about the project was correct but neglected the student element, a tough lesson in a country where over 27 percent of the population is under 19, the highest in Europe. The education team was disappointed due to their commitment to creativity and to inspiring children to be part of a lifelong journey through culture. The lesson learned was to pay attention to the audience, especially when the aspiration to advance artistic excellence and innovation for young people is paramount.

Human situations, such as an interview panel, can provide a different exemplar. What is that "extra something" that leads you to select one person above another? Picture the situation—all the candidates have been interviewed for a job, their qualities, skills and abilities assessed on a score card. Two candidates emerge in the running. When the panel makes the final decision, someone speaks about feeling instinctively that one candidate was more suitable than the other. When asked to explain, they list the qualities on the score card, but admit that in their judgment, candidate X and not Y was a better fit for the museum post. Does that sound familiar?

Another instance is that of the group dynamic. Do you recall being part of a project or an exhibition team when a decision had to be made at a critical point, e.g., can the curator reduce the number of works in the exhibition, where is funding to be sourced for a marketing campaign, why is the catalogue design unappealing? These are crunch moments when everyone feels stressed. No one is prepared to speak—until someone ventures a solution, which leads to another and gradually the problem melts away. When the meeting is over, how many times have you heard someone say "he/she used good judgment by making suggestions at just the right moment and look how the issue was resolved." The likelihood is that the person's training and experience helped to inform a sense of good judgment.

The example of going with a strong instinct was what motivated publication of a book called *Discover Irish Art,* which was created following the appointment of a new curator of Irish art. It could have been written anytime, but a sense that now was the moment provided the catalyst, augmented by a new interest in Irish art, at a time when contemporary issues of "Irishness" and identity had surfaced in Irish society. It proved to be a good judgment call becuase the book sold out and went into reprint.

Good judgment can also come from the simple experience of observing visitors on the museum floor. Noticing patterns, such as the numbers of families visiting the museum, apparently with nothing to do, or people in later life who become tired as they wander around the galleries at a loss to know what to make of the collections. The outcome of the observations was the creation of "Family Kits" (discovery trails and drawing equipment) for families to borrow and use together, and "Art Packs" (self-guides, highlights of the collection and practical activities) for older adults to use in the galleries. The same type of instinct guided hesitant museums to branch into digital media only to be galvanized into action by observing the speed with which the younger generation used the Internet and social networking. As a result, new technology has become an essential tool for museums in the 21st century. These examples amply demonstrate the successful use of good judgment in addressing situations.

The final case in point illustrates the use of both judgment and instinct at a particular time. This occurred when the board of the Irish Museums Association realized there was a need to raise awareness about museums among the Irish public. They decided instinctively to seize the moment and act swiftly. The outcome was the mounting of a touring exhibition accompanied by a catalogue, online material for young people and an outreach program. The most difficult task was to obtain joint funding from the north and the south of Ireland to ensure the project was an all-island one. The exhibition also had to reflect collections from every corner of the country, and there was no way of knowing how it would be received. In the end, instinct, determination and a hard-working board that succeeded in obtaining the funding won the day. The exhibition, "Museums Matter: Accessing Ireland's Heritage," was launched in Dublin and Belfast and immediately embarked on a tour of Ireland. This example shows the outcome of employing instinct to guide an initiative, together with good judgment in assessing the risks.

What often emerges from these situations are the friendships with colleagues who stand by you when things do and don't work out. When Samuel Beckett said, "Ever failed. No matter. Try again. Fail again. Fail better,"[3] he understood that failure sharpens one's awareness of what went wrong and enables you to draw from this experience when developing new ideas. The ability to succeed and fail and to learn from these experiences helps to develop a person's instinct for knowing when to sieze that moment.

Seamus Heaney wrote, "To an imaginative person, an inherited object... is not just an object, an antique, an item on an inventory; rather it becomes a point of entry into a common emotional ground of memory and belonging." He could have been referring to a time in our lives when we seized the moment by using good judgment to act on our instincts. He concludes, "The more we are surrounded by such objects and are attentive to them, the more richly and contentedly we dwell in our own lives."[4] This encapsulates some of the benefits of working in the museum.

Endnotes

1.   James Joyce, *A Portrait of the Artist as a Young Man* (New York: B. W. Heubsch, 1916), conclusion.

2.   Paul Durcan, "preface" to *Crazy about Women* (Dublin: National Gallery of Ireland, 1991), x-xi.

3.   Samuel Beckett, *Worstward Ho 1983*, published 1989 (London: collected in Nowhow On: Company, Ill Seen Ill Said, Worstward Ho, Grove Press, 1995).

4.   Seamus Heaney, "A Sense of the Past," *History Ireland*, vol. 1, no. 4, winter, 1993, p. 33–37.

Afterword

Caitlin Kreiman Lill

Environmental Office Manager, Urbana Park District

I was graduating with my master's degree in museum studies just as I was hired at my current job. I had taken a year off after college to work and get some experience, but had never really doubted that I wanted a graduate degree. I am someone who needs structure to study; I learn best when there are deadlines, requirements and opportunities for hands-on experiences. Knowing these things about myself helped me pick the right program, along with financial and job-prospect considerations.

The advice from Ben Garcia (Chapter 15) resonates with my experience of why graduate school was the right decision for me. I personally chose the more generic museum studies degree as opposed to museum education or administrative programs, despite knowing that I wanted to be an education manager—and later, director—at a museum. Just as he said, I was looking for the "big ideas" that I could apply to a variety of experiences, and didn't want to specialize just yet.

The most amazing thing I've found post-graduation is the immediate applicability of my studies to the daily work that I'm doing. My position includes fundraising, and I was lucky to have had several grant-writing internships through my program. I'm also involved in curriculum development and lesson planning, for which my formal education classes have provided consistent guidance. The best part, though, is that my thesis research into education departmental planning has transformed from feeling like a "safe" choice of topics to an irreplaceable part of my current work. Almost the second I stepped foot in my museum, I started working on an education plan with the staff and board. Looking back on the many conversations I had with my advisers before picking a topic, I'm amazed at how effortlessly they steered me towards a topic with such immediate tangible benefits to my career.

While I ultimately loved the program I went through, I do wish someone had told me one thing Garcia mentioned: to seek out a studies program whose professors or alumni are people you admire. If you have the opportunity, and know what type of experience you're looking for, I strongly recommend following this advice and taking a thorough look at the professors and graduates from the programs you're considering.

Even after just a few months at my new job, I can also relate to the importance of Elee Wood's essay (Chapter 16). As a new manager, I've found myself putting in far more than 40 hours per week to keep up with my steep learning curve, and I can see how that work style could become a natural habit. While I've never thought that museum work was contained in a neat 8 a.m.–5 p.m. day (especially in education), that doesn't mean a salaried position should be 60-plus hours every week. At some point I'll need to adjust to what I've called a "new normal," in which I perform my job with dedication and passion but without sacrificing my life outside of work to complete it. Learning to accept that there are boundaries in what could be a never-ending job is difficult, and I'll admit that I haven't found my balance yet. One of the best things to remember is that burning out, or sacrificing too much to your career, will be more harmful to your institution than helpful.

While I'm more than fortunate to have a museum job that perfectly matches my interests, I already wonder what I should do next. Solid, continuous experience in my job is a clear priority for me, as I'm confident I can learn more through work right now than I could through additional schooling. In the back of my mind, though, is wisdom like that from Marie Bourke (Chapter 17), and a strong desire to reach the level of intuitive judgment that she describes. Most of this, as she says, just comes with time and experience, meaning that patience is the key component. Because there are more rungs in the ladder, I have to wonder if a Ph.D., M.B.A. or certifications are in my future.

Remember that your career isn't meant to be a simple checklist of experiences that will lead you to retirement. Museum education is a creative, stimulating pursuit that often allows you to witness personal transformations in yourself and others. Those of us who are emerging educators often need help in establishing where our boundaries are, how formal and informal education opportunities can advance our own careers and how to develop an intuitive grasp of the discipline. The essays by Garcia, Wood and Bourke provide inspiring and lasting advice on these three issues, and I will certainly reference them for years to come.

Things to Ponder:

1. Consider the underlying drive for your work in museum education. What type of work energizes and stimulates you? What type of work challenges you?

2. Can you recall a time when you or your colleagues failed with a program or outreach activity? What did you learn from the experience? Did the experience change your approach to future efforts?

Then, Now, Next:
Transferring a Lifetime of Careers

Greg Stevens

Assistant Director for Professional Development,
American Alliance of Museums

"Nothing endures but change."
—Heraclitus (c. 535 B.C.–475 B.C.)

I n my 10-plus years in the museum world and more than
25 years in my successive careers as a theater designer,
elementary school arts educator, museum educator and
professional development specialist (along with several long-ago
years of waiting tables, bartending and catering gigs thrown in
for survival), I've had the great fortune to work in a variety of
environments, on a good many types of projects and programs,
and with or for a range of smart, talented, passionate and committed individuals. In each of what I call my "career lifetimes," I
have in various amounts:

- gotten as much as (if not more than) I've given

- learned as much as (if not more than) I've taught

- observed as often as taken action

- learned to listen more and talk less

- (frequently) spoken up when a case needed to be made

- made more good decisions than not-so-good

- celebrated successes along with "growth opportunities"

I anticipate I'll continue along this spectrum for the next two decades of my professional life—learning, giving, stumbling and growing along. As I think about my work as an aspiring, emerging and now mid-career museum professional, and the field to which I have committed, I find myself having created a reflective philosophy of practice that guides me through the sometimes daily twists and turns of my career. In considering the many things I have observed, experienced and learned over the years, I have arranged them unscientifically into three broad "career lifetimes" that I call "Then, Now, Next."

Then

I'm frequently asked by emerging museum colleagues how I got to where I am in my career. My answer is fairly straightforward and equally oblique: you never know how your life and career will unfold. Who I am and where I come from informs where and how I've landed (so far), and influences my values, behavior, work ethic and how I communicate with myself and others.

For example, my imagination has always been highly active and highly visible. As a kid I used to borrow my mom's bedroom drapes to make curtains for the puppet stage I made from Christmas lights and the refrigerator box I had just dragged home from the appliance shop down the street. This creative play and my early interest in art, storytelling and theater (Picasso, Shakespeare, science fiction and *The Wizard of Oz* were all heavy influencers) led to a theater career—first as an actor, then as a set and costume designer. This led to a decade-long career designing and teaching art and theater at a performing and visual arts elementary school in San Diego, which led to my awareness that I'm a good teacher (but wasn't interested in being a classroom teacher per se) and that teaching is like being on stage! This led to my cross-country journey to Washington, DC, and the Museum Education Program (MEP) at The George Washington University, which led to my career as a museum educator and now as a professional development specialist at the American Alliance of Museums (the Alliance).

Early on in my museum career, I started developing a growing sense of self as a museum professional and felt compelled to help other colleagues explore their own identities and career paths, in part to help me make sense of some of the decisions I had made in my chosen career. Although I had come to museum work by way of the MEP and had spent rewarding years as a museum educator, I found myself gravitating toward adult learners and career development. I began creating workshops, sessions and seminars designed to help participants explore their individual strengths and passions as critical to their professional happiness and success. In the process, I learned a great deal about myself, and was surprised to know of the many and varied paths my colleagues traveled to get to museum work. I realized that I am simultaneously unique but not so different from many other museum professionals. It was in these early years of my museum career that I started to establish a keen understanding of and passion for concepts and topics that would grow to shape my current work.

Another significant revelation was the relationship between my former career as a theater professional and my new career as a museum professional. When I came to museum work, I divorced myself from my theater background, not recognizing that nearly everything I am, know how to do and care most about I learned from the theater, i.e., creating something that never existed before; sharing ideas and concepts with talented, creative people; working hard, collaborating, facing deadlines; and knowing that no matter what, "the show must go on" (even if the set is still wet with paint and the costumes are held together with safety pins!). Now more than ever, I reflect on my theater work and realize how important it was and still is to my daily work in planning, implementing and evaluating professional development programs with and for colleagues in the museum field.

Now

Most of the people with whom I work and engage in various capacities tell me that their decision to embrace museum work has to do with (variations on) a love of art, history, objects, ideas, science, kids, families, communities, nature, animals and/or education. I've never had anyone tell me they came to museum work to make lots of money. What I do see and experience from my colleagues is a career commitment to excellence, fueled by a love of lifelong learning, skills building, reflective practice, recognition of the power of professional relationships and passion. One way I attempt to honor and share this commitment is to focus on helping colleagues build a stronger personal brand, which I summarize here and talk more about in *A Life in Museums: Managing Your Museum Career* (2012, The AAM Press). In brief, your personal brand is:

- knowing what you're good at

- knowing what you're passionate about

- communicating your skills and passions in distinctive, relevant and consistent ways

What I'm good at and passionate about are generally one and the same—coming up with ideas, and putting people and resources together to make something happen that never existed before, something of value and impact. My skills and passions play out differently under different circumstances and with different stakeholders, but I am lucky to work in a job and field that generally celebrates my skills and passions. Still I am constantly learning how *intent* and *perception* are two sides of the same communication dynamic, and so I strive to improve my process and product through a continual 360-degree feedback loop with co-workers and colleagues.

The success of the teams and project groups with whom I collaborate is influenced by our individual and collective ability to dream, engage, create, innovate, communicate, collaborate, push back, disagree, reconcile, move on, commit, trust, change, adapt and love. This is a lofty statement and goal, but one that is essential to my work. It serves as the bedrock of my philosophy of practice. In short, I believe our individual contributions (words and deeds) have a direct impact on our institutions, our communities (and communities of practice), our field as a whole, and how we speak with one voice about why and how museums are essential components of the global learning landscape. Graphically it looks like the following, which, as a visual learner, I find easy to recall and reference:

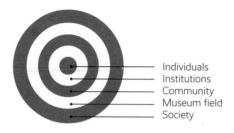

When I was in graduate school at GWU, we were encouraged to advocate for our profession, our visitors and our field by getting involved. I recall asking MEP Program Director Carol Stapp about the ways in which we might we get involved beyond our primary jobs. Her response, which resonates for me with lasting clarity and prescience, was simple and to the point: "Raise your hand." I carry this message with me and promote it whenever, wherever and to whomever possible. We all have something of value to offer to our colleagues, our institutions, our visitors, the field and society.

To put a practical spin on the topic, consider for yourself how any of the following activities might align with your unique passions and skills, and how each might help you communicate your personal brand while giving back to the field. In whatever ways you choose to engage, do so with purpose and full awareness of your commitment (read: give 150 percent).

- Join a professional association; if the Alliance seems too big, try your state or regional association.

- Join a local group in your city or region, like the Alliance's Emerging Museum Professionals (EMPs), or raise your hand to start one if one doesn't yet exist.

- Join a national committee like the Alliance's Committee on Education Professional Network (EdCom).

- Write an article for your school's or museum's monthly newsletter.

- Submit an article to the Alliance's *Museum* magazine.

- Submit a session proposal to the Alliance Annual Meeting; if this seems too big, try your state or regional museum conference.

- Volunteer at a local museum, theater or other cultural center.

- Get or be a mentor to a colleague.

- Sharpen your professional skills by keeping up with the literature, attending a seminar or workshop, participating in a webinar or presenting at a conference.

- Network by building relationships with colleagues at your job, in your local community, in your region and beyond.

To this last point, think about the previous "bull's eye" graphic as a framework for networking. "Networking" is a frequently mis- or over-used term, and I've found it is not well understood or practiced by many of my colleagues. In truth, networking is nothing more than *identifying and building mutually beneficial relationships,* some of which may be short-term or long-term. I can't overemphasize the importance of strong colleague relationships as you go through your career. True networking takes work, true give-and-take, and generous attitude and action. The rewards are worth the effort. People like those with whom they have a strong emotional connection, and you foster this connection by demonstrating your *personal brand* (i.e., being distinctive, relevant and consistent in all you do and say).

Next

It may sound like a cliché, but your career is entirely in your control even though there may be times when you feel less than in control of given circumstances. For example, you may have a great job but a lousy boss. You have choices about how you manage this situation; it might be time to address your skills and/or attitude to improve your performance, or it may be time for you to move on. Maybe you got laid off from your job as part of a reduction in force or other organizational shift; you can wallow or you can get to it and volunteer while you look for another job. You may have been in your job for many years and need a new challenge, or you may be in your job only a year or two and have learned everything you need to learn and it's time to move on. If that's the case, then do it (but be mindful of not burning bridges).

The workforce and workplace are changing across the landscape, and museums are no exception. It is not news in our field that aspiring colleagues right out of school are having a tough time finding jobs. Many younger colleagues coming into the workforce will stay in any given job for only a couple of years and may ultimately have over a dozen careers in their lifetimes. At the same time, some of our baby boomer and "Gen X" colleagues are likely to stay in jobs longer (boomers are now working longer than expected into their "retirement years" because of the weak economy). These and other factors make it more critical than ever for museum colleagues to build strong relationships—for now and for the future.

We each have the opportunity and the obligation to "pay it forward" and "give back" to our colleagues and the field by engaging as leaders and/or change agents, for our colleagues, the field and ourselves. One way of doing this is what my colleague Anne Ackerson calls building a "career posse," a trusted group of like-minded folks who get together to think and talk about their careers and the field, past, present and future. These colleagues help each other take stock of their strengths and growth opportunities, help create personal mission and vision statements for their career next-steps (i.e., a "personal career map") and then support each other in putting these plans in action. I'm a firm believer in looking at where you've been and where you are now to help inform what's next. I encourage you to gather a "career posse" of your own. You may already have one in your midst.

Parting Thoughts: Being a Change Agent

In the world of museology, we have seen a progressive, if not always fully embraced shift over time in our definition of, philosophy about and practice of "museum"—from a cabinet of curiosities to a communal place of learning and experience. The various and collective aspects of our lives as museum professionals suggest that how we interact with each other, how we engage our communities, how we do our work and to what purpose are invariably the result of someone making change happen. Names like John Cotton Dana, Bonnie Pitman, Elaine Heumann Gurian and Steve Weil all come to mind. There are many others. You may be one of them.

Change agents by definition are first and foremost passionate, self-motivated, resilient individuals who understand people on a fundamental level and systems on a higher plane. A change agent has a vision of what could or should be and uses that as the guiding principle(s) toward action. Change agents are leaders (with the acknowledgment that not all leaders are change agents), willing to take bold steps, knowing that the path might be messy and inconvenient with few clear-cut answers and frequent pushback.

Being a reflective practitioner and lifelong learner and forging creative connections with skill, passion and commitment are essential elements of being a museum change agent as leader. Are you that change agent? Are *you* prepared to "raise your hand?"

Contributors

Sarah Alvarez is director of Teacher Programs at the Art Institute of Chicago. She holds an M.A. in art history and has been at the museum since 2001. Alvarez began her tenure at the Art Institute in adult programming, teaching extensively on all areas of the collection. Since 2008, Alvarez has directed the museum's teacher programs division, offering a comprehensive professional development program of workshops and printed and electronic resources for pre-K–12 educators in Chicago and beyond. Sarah continues to work with medical students on honing perception and observation skills through looking at art.

Sheri Bernstein is vice president and director of education at the Skirball Cultural Center, where she is responsible for the creation, facilitation and evaluation of all offerings for students, teachers and families. She oversees the Skirball's school programs, serving pre-K–12 students and teachers, and the related docent-touring program. As project director of "Noah's Ark at the Skirball," a family destination that received a 2008 Excellence in Exhibition award from AAM, Bernstein led the project's core team and now oversees its programs, staffing and operations. She holds degrees from Yale University and Harvard University.

Marie Bourke, Ph.D. is keeper and head of education at the National Gallery of Ireland. She researches, lectures and writes. Publications include *The Story of Irish Museums 1790–2000* (2011), *Discover Irish Art* (co-author, 1999); *Art in Transition* (1998) and *Exploring Art* (1997). A former chair of the Irish Museums Association, she is coordinator of the LEM Working Group "New Trends in Museums of the 21st Century," and adjunct professor, School of Cultural Policy & Art History, University College, Dublin.

William Crow is managing museum educator of School and Teacher Programs at the Metropolitan Museum of Art. He is assistant professor of museum studies at New York University and adjunct instructor at Johns Hopkins University. He co-authored *Unbound by Place or Time: Museums and Online Learning* (2009) and *All Together Now: Museums and Online Collaborative Learning* (2010), both published by The AAM Press. He holds a B.A. in Romance languages and art from Wake Forest, an M.F.A. in painting from The City University of New York and an M.S.Ed. in museum education leadership from Bank Street, and is completing his Ph.D. in cognition at Teachers College, Columbia University.

Celeste DeWald was introduced to museum work about 20 years ago when she helped develop a mobile art museum that traveled to elementary schools. She became fascinated with the vibrant educational role museums can play in bringing the arts, humanities and science to life for audiences. Since that time, she has worked as the curator or director of education in museums, graduated from John F. Kennedy University with an M.A. in museum studies, and has served as the executive director of the California Association of Museums for 10 years.

Paula Gangopadhyay is the chief learning officer for The Henry Ford, which includes the Henry Ford Museum, Greenfield Village, Benson Ford Research Center, Ford Rouge Factory Tour, IMAX and Henry Ford Academy. She brings more than 18 years of experience in the education, policy and cultural sectors. President Obama appointed Gangopadhyay a member of the National Board of Museums and Libraries in 2012 for a four-year term. She is the recipient of the 2012 American Alliance of Museums' EdCom Award for Excellence in Practice. She was recently appointed to the board of the Henry Ford Academy.

Ben Garcia is head of interpretation at the Phoebe A. Hearst Museum of Anthropology at UC-Berkeley. His previous museum experience includes teaching and administrative roles in the education departments of the J. Paul Getty Museum and Skirball Cultural Center. He serves on the development committee for the National Art Education Association's museum division and on the board of the Adoption Museum Project. His publications and presentations have focused on museum education as it relates to public value and social change. In 2010 he was named Pacific Region Museum Art Educator of the Year by the National Art Education Association.

Brad Irwin has worked in the education sector for over 15 years. His experience covers both formal and informal settings, having worked as a primary school teacher, university lecturer, gallery interpreter and gallery education manager. He is currently the senior learning engagement manager at the Natural History Museum, London, where he is responsible for all learning engagement teams, including 26 science educators and 100 learning volunteers. He is particularly interested in embedding current informal learning research into practice. He is the author of a children's book entitled *Let's Get Art* (Random House, 2008) examining contemporary New Zealand art.

Katarina Ivanišin Kardum was born in Dubrovnik. In 2000 she graduated in fine art painting from the Royal College of Art in London. Since then, she has worked as an artist and part-time lecturer at City & Guilds of London Art School. She worked as a museum educator in the re-opened Dubrovnik Natural History Museum, where she authored several publications and educational programs, such as the catalogue for children, *Protected Species* and the exhibitions "How Big Was the Tuna in Our Museum?" and "*Dermochelys coriacea*." She currently creates educational programs for the Technical Museum in Zagreb.

Caitlin Kreiman Lill is an emerging museum professional working as the environmental office manager with the Urbana Park District in Illinois. After graduating with a B.A. in biology and classics from Beloit College, she went on to receive her M.A. in museum studies from San Francisco State University. She has also worked with the Museum of the Grand Prairie, Hayward Area Historical Society, Sacramento Zoo, CuriOdyssey and the Logan Museum of Anthropology. Lill has been actively involved with the

Emerging Museum Professionals movement through the American Alliance of Museums.

Recently retired, **Ted Lind** served as a museum educator for 32 years. He held positions at the Philadelphia Museum of Art, the Albany Institute of History & Art, the Cincinnati Art Museum and the Newark Museum. Lind is a visual artist, and taught studio art and art history at the college level before engaging in museum education. He has written and spoken extensively on subjects related to the role of museums in teaching and learning. Lind also served as vice chair of the Education Committee of the American Alliance of Museums. He currently resides in Granville Ferry, Nova Scotia.

Museum and science educator **Sarah Marcotte** has been contributing to the field for 18 years. A graduate of the Bank Street master's in museum education program, Marcotte has worked at the Natural History Museum of Los Angeles County and Kidspace Children's Museum in southern California. She has served on the boards of the Museum Educators of Southern California, the Museum Education Roundtable, and AAM's Media and Technology Professional Network. She currently works for the Mars Exploration program at NASA's Jet Propulsion Laboratory, providing resources about current Mars missions to science centers and planetariums.

Lynn McRainey is the chief education officer and Elizabeth F. Cheney Director of Education at the Chicago History Museum. A leader in institutional advancement and audience accessibility, she chaired the visioning committee, directed the development of award-winning interpretive experiences and initiated institutional planning for family audiences. Co-editor and chapter author of *Connecting Kids to History with Museum Exhibitions*, McRainey served on the editorial advisory board and was guest editor for the *Journal of Museum Education*. She has been a guest instructor at Bank Street and delivered the keynote address for the Museum & Gallery Services annual conference (Queensland, Australia). McRainey has received fellowships from the NEH and the Smithsonian.

Leah M. Melber, Ph.D. is senior director of the Hurvis Center for Learning Innovation and Collaboration at Lincoln Park Zoo, Chicago. She brings over 20 years of experience in informal and formal science education. She holds a B.A. in zoology, an M.A. and a Ph.D. in educational psychology from the University of Southern California. Her presentations and refereed publications focus on improving public understanding of scientific research through effective program design within informal learning environments. She was awarded the 2010 Promising Leadership Award by the Association of Midwest Museums.

Marjorie Schwarzer is administrative director and a faculty member at the University of San Francisco's graduate museum studies program. She is author of AAM's best-selling book, *Riches, Rivals and Radicals: 100 Years of Museums in America* (2006; 2012), as well as numerous articles on the museum field. She began her museum career as a graduate student intern at the Berkeley Art Museum in 1981 and has held leadership positions at John F. Kennedy University, Boston Children's Museum, Chicago Children's Museum and Chicago's Museum of Science and Industry.

Beverly Serrell, director of Serrell & Associates, has been an exhibit and evaluation consultant with art, history, natural history and science museums, as well as with zoos and aquariums, since 1979. She headed the museum education department at the Shedd Aquarium for eight years and had shorter stints as a high school teacher and research lab technician. She holds an M.A. in science teaching in informal settings and a B.S. in biology. In 1995 she was a guest scholar at the J. Paul Getty Museum, and in 1996 and 2002 Serrell & Associates was awarded National Science Foundation grants to study visitors and museum exhibitions.

K. Tierney Sneeringer credits her art teachers, a sense of adventure and love of different cultures for her decision to study art history and Spanish at the University of Delaware. Sneeringer went on to receive her M.A.T. in museum education from The George Washington University. She currently works at the Smithsonian American Art Museum's Luce Foundation Center for American Art. Sneeringer has worked on a variety of projects at the Luce Center, but most notably has started and manages two programs that feature local artists and musicians. She is always looking for new ways to engage local communities in museum settings.

Greg Stevens has directed the American Alliance of Museums' professional development program since 2007, including international and advocacy programs, Professional Network programs, seminars and webinars, Emerging Museum Professional initiatives and AAM Career Café. Previously Stevens held education positions at the National Museum of the U.S. Army, Mid-Atlantic Association of Museums, National Building Museum and Smithsonian National Air and Space Museum. He earned his M.A.T., museum education, from The George Washington University and his B.A. in theater from San Diego State University. Stevens is the co-editor (with Wendy Luke) of *A Life in Museums: Managing Your Museum Career* (The AAM Press, 2012).

Kathleen Tinworth is the founder and principal at ExposeYourMuseum LLC, a consulting firm helping cultural organizations to better understand their current and potential visitors, communities and audiences. Tinworth has more than 12 years of experience designing, developing and executing professional research and evaluation. She combines audience research, strategic illustration, market analysis, user-centered design, capacity building and community empowerment to transform organizations. From 2007–2013, Tinworth led the department of Audience Insights at the Denver Museum of Nature & Science.

Elizabeth (Elee) Wood, Ph.D is an associate professor at Indiana University-Purdue University, Indianapolis. She serves as the director of the museum studies program, with a joint appointment in education, and serves as public scholar of museums, families and learning at The Children's Museum of Indianapolis. Her research interests include object-based learning, community-based learning and critical museum pedagogies. Wood teaches courses in museum education, museums and audiences, museum theater and object-based learning. She got her museum start early as a youth interpreter in the Wizard Wing, Milwaukee Public Museum, and worked as a museum exhibit developer, program manager and evaluator.

Index